THE STORY OF REX OF WHITE WAY
The Blizzard King

THE BOOK

by

Jim Cheskawich

Samoyed Club of America,
former president and treasurer;
Samoyed Club of America Education and
Research Foundation, treasurer;
Willamette Valley Samoyed Fanciers,
treasurer and former president;
American Kennel Club Breeder of Merit®
Registered Trademark Participant

Rex With His Best Friend, Trainer Lloyd Van Sickle.

REX

In the early days of black-and-white TV in the 1950s, while Lassie, Rin-Tin-Tin, and even *Superman* received most of their public acclaim in "reel life," Rex of White Way served as a hero in "real life." Born on September 26, 1946, he was internationally known from about age two onwards for his exploits... and his adventures. In a day when there were no snowmobiles, Rex was called *"The Blizzard King"* because of his ability to make a path through blinding snow.

He performed over 30 arduous, sled-dog "rescue missions," including his most famous: The "Modern-Day Donner Party" Rescue in 1952, when he led the White Way Team carrying Doctor Lawrence D. Nelson to stranded passengers aboard the snowbound train, *City of San Francisco*. As you will also read in the Rex story, just like *Superman*, Rex routinely jumped through windows, and at one point was considered "The Strongest Dog on the Planet." He also "starred" in an episode of the popular TV show, "Have Gun Will Travel," and was "on the set" as "guard dog" to John Wayne during the filming of *Island in the Sky* in Lake Tahoe. The Duke was so taken with Rex that he kept him on location for three additional months to have someone to "pal around with."

We all need heroes to admire and serve as role models in overcoming life's difficulties. Not considered good enough to meet the "standard" for the dog-show world's "Conformation Ring," because he was over the height standard, his coat was too short, and he had those four long, gangly legs that "looked like they came out of one socket," he was sent out to trainer Lloyd Van Sickle to "make himself useful." Rex did much more than that! He became a figure larger than life.

Rex is every man or woman or child who has been told he or she "doesn't have what it takes," and yet somehow through hard work and hidden talent makes it in a huge way! I hope you enjoy the story of Rex and his adventures through life. He was truly the epitome of "man's best friend" and an inspiring example of why dogs are so universally loved.

REX, STANDING TALL! NOTICE HIS LONG LEGS. ONCE CONSIDERED A "LIABILITY," REX TRANSFORMED THIS IMAGE BY USING HIS LONG LEGS TO BLAZE TRAILS THROUGH HIGH SNOWDRIFTS AS THE LEADER OF RESCUE TEAMS.

THE STORY OF REX OF WHITE WAY

The Blizzard King

THE BOOK

BY

JIM CHESKAWICH

REX THE BLIZZARD KING STORIES, LLC
WOODLAND, WASHINGTON
2012

The Story of Rex of White Way, The Blizzard King—**The Book**

FIRST EDITION

ISBN (Hardback) 978-0-9883640-0-4
ISBN (Paperback) 978-0-9883640-1-1

Library of Congress LCCN: 2012919853

Grateful appreciation for use of Pictures, and Excerpts from Interviews with Lloyd Van Sickle, used by permission of Steve Van Sickle.

Thank you to Carol Chittum, Belaya Samoyeds, for use of her extensive photographic library.

Thank you to Michael Kanyon, Kanyon Films, for use of his archival photographic collection.

Primary Sources, used by permission: *Western Kennel World* magazine (*WKW*) 1938–1958 issues; *Samoyed Club of America Bulletin* (*SCA*) 1945–2011 issues; *American Kennel Club Gazette* (*AKC*) February 2008; Original pages and photos, Gertrude Adams Private Collection (1910–1970); *Organization for the Working Samoyed Newsletter* (*OWS*), *The Yapper*, August 1972; *The Samoyed Quarterly* (*SQ*) 1977–2008 issues; Samoyed Club of America Historical Archives; *Northern Dog News* (*NDN*), December 1974.

Special acknowledgment to Nan Holt for use of her original artwork, "Rescue at Yuba Gap," winner, "Best in Art Show" at the SCA 2012 National.

Front cover photos, courtesy Lloyd and Steve Van Sickle. Back cover photo, courtesy Kay Ketchum, Lloyd and Alta Van Sickle.

Author photo, Minette Siegel.

Printed in the U.S.A. by:
Modern Litho, Jefferson City, MO

A portion of the proceeds from sales of this book will go toward sustaining a Rex of White Way Memorial Library, providing for the operational costs of a Rex of White Way website, and making educational contributions for Agnes Mason's grandchildren and great-grandchildren.

Published by
Rex The Blizzard King Stories, LLC
183 Wieri Road, Woodland, WA 98674
Phone: 360-225-8402 • Fax: 360-225-0422
E-Mail: samtres@earthlink.net
Website: http://dketasamoyeds.com

DEDICATION

To Agnes Mason and Aljean Mason Larson; to Rex; and to Lloyd, Alta, Steve, and Sandy Van Sickle and Sara Van Sickle Dexter, because without their close teamwork, we don't have a story.

To Brutus, a mixed breed "mountain of a dog," who usually helped me guard the bunker line at night when it was my shift while serving in Phu Bai, South Vietnam in 1971, and the friend of many in the 101st Airborne Division.

To Edmund Raymond Sledzik, American Kennel Club Delegate and Dog Show Judge, Tax Attorney, and card player who taught me how to play gin in Hawaii in between writing the first Rex book chapters and making trips to Costco for Dove Ice Cream Bars dipped in chocolate and crushed almonds.

And to Ch. Oakbrook's Strike It Rich ("Ono"), who always made me feel I was in the company of royalty when I was around him, and whose bloodline flows from the ancient Samoyeds [from] Rex...and on through the Samoyed breed today.

Each age, it is found, must write its own books;
or rather,
each generation for the next succeeding.

RALPH WALDO EMERSON
FROM THE AMERICAN SCHOLAR ORATION, DELIVERED
BEFORE THE PHI BETA KAPPA SOCIETY, HARVARD UNIVERSITY, CAMBRIDGE, MA
AUGUST 31, 1837.

DOG SLED ILLUSTRATION ON SLATE BY NAN HOLT.
PHOTOGRAPH BY NOEL JOHNSON.
COURTESY JIM CHESKAWICH.

ACKNOWLEDGMENTS

I thank Michael Kanyon, Kanyon Films, for his originating idea for the story about Rex of White Way, and for use of his archival photograhic collection.

Appreciation is due Celinda Cheskawich for her patience, research, collection of *Western Kennel World* magazines, creativity, and editorial input into the story.

I also want to thank Nan Holt, Brad Johnson, and Pam Landers for their artwork and Noel Johnson for his photography. I appreciate the encouragement and comments along the way from Edmond Raymond and Carolyn Sledzik, Amelia Price, Pam Barbe, Sheila Goffe, Dr. Susan Crockford, Mark McLaughlin, Mike Blide, Colleen Dallam, Helen Corlew Newman, David, Marion, and Faithie Gustafson, Madelin Druse, Dyllon Humphreys, Carol Chittum, Deb Fiedler, Steven and Susan Amundson, Rudy Munoz, Ross and Sue Chapin, Alan and Jean Clough, Gail Spieker, Dan Moradian, Joan Luna, Christie Smith, Tamara Somerville, Sakura Moses, Mardee Ward-Fanning, Lloyd, Alta, and Steve Van Sickle and Sara Van Sickle Dexter, Kay Ketchum, Pat deBack, Sandie Flettner, Cathy Cusack, Pat Hill Goodrich, Darlu Littledeer, Wilna Coulter, Kathy Mackai, Harold McCoy, PJ (Peggy-Jo) Faria, Lee Brumbaugh, Frank Rossback, Neil Koppes, Ron and Ada Alyward from England, and the many members and friends of the Samoyed community.

Thanks is also to be given my editor, Vicki Weiland, who believed in the book from the beginning, for her encouragement, support, suggestions, and for smoothing out the story. Minette Siegel is singled out for her photographic expertise in bringing the archival collections to clarity and "life." Dawn Pasinski helped greatly in the photographic reproductions, and her faithful transcriptions of the colorful recollections of Lloyd Van Sickle were critically important. Desta Garrett Book Design is to be thanked for production of the cover and interior of the book. Both she and Lynn La of Express Print are appreciated for their contributions producing and mailing out the Mock-Ups, and will be pleased to know that the two Samoyeds in my kennel wildly "serenaded" the UPS delivery truck as the second batch was delivered in late August. Both Samoyeds have Rex as an ancestor, and acted as if they "recognized" a connection.

At Modern Litho, much thanks and appreciation goes to Kim Neidert for being my publisher, along with his team of Monica Peters and Sharon Kliethermes. Modern Litho was my first choice, and Kim was on the phone to me within a few hours of receiving the book Mock-Up! Rex deserves to be treated royally, and every author should be so lucky to find such a responsive and highly capable team.

Thanks also to all the students in the Battle Ground, Green Mountain, and La Center School Districts in Southwest Washington State who served as my captive audience and allowed me to tell them Rex "stories" and gave me feedback while serving as a substitute teacher in between the lesson plan readings for Dr. Seuss, Jan Brett, Kurt Vonnegut, Geoffrey Chaucer, Ray Bradbury, or Jack London. Teaching music for K–2 at La Center Elementary School recently and playing the "Sorcerer's Apprentice" (Paul Dukas-composer) throughout the day, inspired me to include the story about my own Samoyed, Riley (a descendant of Rex's), and his win in 2011 as "Best in Show."

I apologize to the 4th grade class at La Center Elementary School when I outlined a story several years ago to show you how to outline a story for your writing class, as I inadvertently mixed up the details of Rex's crashed plane rescue in Truckee, California with his delivery of the medical doctor to provide relief to the snowbound train passengers stuck in the High Sierra's aboard the *City of San Francisco.*

Without the reminiscences and pictures willingly provided by Lloyd, Alta, and Steve Van Sickle, much of Rex's life and background would still remain hidden. I have tried to be faithful to the facts as they were presented. I am deeply grateful to Lloyd, Rex's trainer, for allowing us to interview him in March 2004. Lloyd passed away on December 27, 2006 at the age of 88 from double pneumonia, so he now is reunited with his beloved, great lead dog.

I am also grateful for the suggestions, story input or interview recollections provided by Aljean Mason Larson, Alice Lombardi, Jim Osborn, and Lee and Mel Fishback. I am particularly indebted for substantive subject matter advice and rewriting to Helen Corlew Newman for sledding and Dr. Susan Crockford for dog origins, respectively.

I left in my Rex story the *skijoring* incident of many years ago involving Rex and then-teenager Jerry Brown (who became Governor of California), to show just how Rex "got around" and was "a force of Nature." That's one way to look at Rex! Rex also led the dog sled team that "took out" part of the pillar of the Capitol Building in Sacramento, California.

The Samoyed Club of America (SCA) has a wealth of well informed and knowledgeable members who provided feedback and advice along the way in the story formulation. Walt Kazularich exhibited a photo album which he took to the SCA National in Escondido, California in 1998. There were several pictures that Walt had of Rex at the races or weight pulls which kept me interested in finding out more of Rex. Files of Gertrude Adams were made available to me from Carol Chittum around 2003, which provided much background information on Agnes Mason, Samoyeds, Rex, and the times.

Carol Chittum, Belaya Samoyeds, willingly lent us her photo library, which provided many original pictures for the Rex story and helped jump start the research on the Rex story.

Along the trail to rediscovering Rex, I went through my own substantial library of Samoyed and dog related books including the Robert and Dolly Ward book, *The New Complete Samoyed*. The Ward book is considered by many to be the "Bible" on Samoyeds. It contains many fascinating stories, pictures, and references on Rex.

Finally, I thank all the Samoyeds that I have been acquainted with or lived with me in my home: Multi-BISS Riley, Multi-BISS Seattle, Multi-BISS Ono, General, Rebel, Samantha, Cricket, Honor, Tacoma, Faith, Noah, Maze, and Gabriella, who all served as a constant source of inspiration, entertainment, enjoyment, and companionship as I continued on with the writing of the Rex story.

A Samoyed Tribute

You were the sunlight in my life
Together we found true delight
Although my roots of Arctic winds
Still lingered in my heart, at whim

I loved you for the fun we shared
We were a family and you cared
I loved you for the chance you gave
For me to show my breed so brave

I am with you each passing day
As many others come your way
My legacy, please don't forget
High on a mountain top I set.

Susan Amundson
1999

ENGLISH ARTWORK FROM CRUFTS.
PHOTOGRAPH BY JIM CHESKAWICH.
COURTESY JIM CHESKAWICH.

TABLE OF CONTENTS

FOREWORD

by
Alta Van Sickle

Jim has chronicled an engaging story capturing the life and relationship between Lloyd and a very special Samoyed dog named "Rex." The early detail and background provided on Agnes and my husband, Lloyd, sets the stage and allows the reader to more fully appreciate the historical Rex. It may seem easier to start the story with Rex and John Wayne or Rex and Rin-Tin-Tin, but this ignores the very critical roles of the master breeder, trainer, and handler behind Rex.

Without the close business relationship between Agnes and Lloyd and their considerable individual abilities, a Rex never arrives on the scene and hits the ground running, or sledding as the case was. Rex was allowed to reach his full potential because of the love, care, and opportunities provided by Agnes, Lloyd, and their extended families.

The reader should appreciate the political and cultural references provided in the book chapters which serve as snapshots of the late 1940s and 1950s.

Rex and Lloyd were quite a team, and together they performed many successful—sometimes fun—and heroic escapades together. With Rex at lead, I still think Lloyd took us too close to the Upper Mesa Falls once, with me in the sled basket! However, Lloyd trusted Rex to listen to him and we survived to tell Rex stories.

Lloyd and Rex were lifelong friends. When they separated, Rex never seemed the same. It seemed like his spirit was always looking for his friend, Lloyd. Although Rex passed away many, many years ago and Lloyd just a few years ago, Lloyd often spoke of his great companion and Rex's ability to focus, listen, and "get the job done."

Rex would have done anything that my husband asked of him. Their trust in each other was close and mutual. They knew they could depend on each other even under great adversity. Rex proved the working ability of this noble breed and their capability to bond and become a TEAM!

I had the privilege of seeing it all happen and then have presented in this wonderful story! My thanks to Jim and his team for their time, research, and diligence in getting the book to completion. Along the way—thanks to Nan Holt—Rex even won a "Best in Art Show" at the 2012 SCA National in Pennsylvania. Rex never ceases to amaze!

Alta Van Sickle, Lloyd's wife,
Sprague River, Oregon,
October 9, 2012

ALTA VAN SICKLE WITH A VERY CONTENTED REX.

Commentary from Steve Van Sickle, Lloyd's son:

"My dad, Lloyd, and Rex saw their tasks with the clarity of the eyes of a soaring eagle. They were the wind under each other's wings."

Steve Van Sickle, A Screaming Eagle
101st Airborne Division
1st of the 506th in Vietnam

Commentary from Kay Ketchum, retired nurse:

"I was afraid that the world would never hear about these two great spirits and their story of respect amidst great challenges. They brought out the best in each other. Their relationship proved the breed's real purpose, which is that the Samoyed is a working breed as well as man's greatest companion, then, now, and always!

"I was honored to be Lloyd's niece and a friend to Rex as well. I had the privilege of knowing and helping Agnes with her Sams in the later part of her life. As I reminisced over the passage in this book about Rex's music lessons at the piano, I could almost hear Rex singing. Agnes actually had to cut those sessions short to save all of our eardrums, including those of Rex. She rewarded me later with one of Rex's last immediate offspring, King Pin. He was the first born in his litter and quite a clown, who enjoyed playing with my children, Greg and Julia. King Pin lived out his life in grand style with my family. He had many trips to Lake Tahoe, and romps in the deep snow, which he loved. He retained a lot of Rex's spirit and zest for life."

Kay Ketchum
Sacramento, California

d'KETA SAMOYEDS IS THE KENNEL NAME FOR
JIM AND CELINDA CHESKAWICH, CHRISTIE SMITH, AND RYANN GRADY.
WEBSITE: http://dketasamoyeds.com
ARTWORK BY JOANNE CAROLAN, BANANA PATCH STUDIO, HANAPEPE, KAUAI, HI.

A WORD FROM THE AUTHOR

In many ways, it seems as if Rex told his own story and all I had to do was uncover what had been hidden for many decades, make the connections, and perform meticulous research.

My personal story involving me as an "author" started almost a year after Michael Kanyon, Kanyon Films, had acquired a Samoyed puppy from my wife, Celinda, and I in 2002. The next summer he stopped by to visit us on his way up from The Sea Ranch in California to Seattle, Washington. During the course of a gourmet Columbia River salmon dinner prepared by Celinda, we started talking about what a well-trained Samoyed was really capable of doing. Rex of White Way was offered as the model of the top working Samoyed of all time! Yes, others, over time, may have broken his records under better weather conditions, improved diet, or training, but Rex stands out as the prototype of what a working dog—whose function is to assist mankind in meaningful and productive labor—should be capable of performing. Rex didn't just "show up" several times a year for a race or a weight pull.

Rex lived every day to work...and there was little off season.

Michael told us that he wanted to produce a "docu-drama" about Rex, and he asked us to verify some facts, particularly regarding Rex's legendary rescues. Thus began the quest for material on the "Rex story" and his trainer, Lloyd Van Sickle. By the next day after Michael's assignment, we had gone through several boxes of *Western Kennel World* magazines that Celinda had been collecting from the 1940s and 50s.

It was exciting to follow Rex's career, and to read about his breeder, Agnes Mason from Sacramento, California, and the real life rescues, dog sled races, weight pulls, dog shows, and how he earned his name, "Rex, *The Blizzard King*," which subsequently seemed a very appropriate title for this book and the docu-drama.

A MASTER "MUSHER" LLOYD, AND A MASTER "TEAM" WITH REX
AS LEADER, ROUNDING THE BEND IN IDAHO,
WITH ALTA VAN SICKLE AS THE PASSENGER IN THE "BASKET SEAT."

It was with much sadness that I finally read of Rex's passing and of his many memorials in the late 1957 issues of the magazine. At that point, for me, the life seemed to fall out of the *Western Kennel World,* as the heroic "Rex period" was over. I wanted to know more about this dog and why he captured the interest of people so easily.

A SAMPLING OF THE MANY HELPFUL AND INFORMATIVE MAGAZINES.
PHOTOGRAPH BY JIM CHESKAWICH. COURTESY JIM CHESKAWICH.

(LEFT TO RIGHT) JUDGES RUDY MUNOZ AND CHRISTIE SMITH
WITH CELINDA CHESKAWICH AND JIM CHESKAWICH AND
MULTI-BISS SEATTLE, 2007.

Even John Wayne found Rex a compelling companion and kept him on the movie set of *Island in the Sky* long after Rex's work was completed as a "guard dog." Celinda and I were intrigued about Rex and his meteoric rise to the top, and the chase was on to discover and assemble all that we could possibly find on Rex!

I had first heard of Rex from reading Robert and Dolly Ward's book, *The New Complete Samoyed*. It was the vehicle that brought me into the fascinating history of the breed, and in particular the larger than life character named Rex of White Way. Even the name fit him perfectly, as "Rex of White Way" seemed to make him stand out as a special dog from some distant past when times were rougher and yet simpler.

Since I had what was believed to be a mixed Samoyed-Golden Retriever cross at the time, and could have only one dog in my townhouse, I had to wait two more years before I could get a purebred Samoyed. I acquired Samantha in 1991—who I later found out went back to Rex of White Way, as do practically all U.S. bred Samoyeds today!

In his lifetime, Rex was touched by "Hollywood," left his very highly significant genetic contribution to the Samoyed breed, earned "the right of way" on a treacherous U.S. mail run as a contracted "employee," and saved more than a few lives, including his dramatic rescue of a trainload of modern-day passengers trapped on the notorious Donner Summit.

In a way, the story of Rex, and his breeders Agnes and A. E. Mason, his fellow White Way Samoyeds, and his trainer Lloyd Van Sickle is tied into the history of California. These remarkable individuals helped develop California, and worked in the sometimes rugged environment to advance (or rescue) civilization, with Lloyd and Rex leading the way.

It is important to note that Rex is currently under consideration by the U.S. Citizen Stamp Advisory Committee for a postage stamp in his honor in recognition of his contributions to the betterment of mankind. He has also appeared in the U.S. Congressional Record (September 22, 2005) honoring his achievements on the occasion of the 74th Samoyed Club of America (SCA) National Specialty held in Owensboro, Kentucky.

As a former SCA president (1999–2001 and 2009–2010), assistant SCA historian, SCA treasurer for many years, co-breeder and exhibitor of Samoyeds along with Celinda, and currently Willamette Valley Samoyed Fanciers treasurer and SCA Foundation treasurer, I have enjoyed pulling the Rex story together and watching offshoots develop, such as the SCA Foundation Greeting Card project, the U.S. stamp request for Rex, Rex's appearance in the Congressional Record, the six page write-up on Samoyeds in the February 2008 *AKC Gazette* (with the lead article about Rex), the SCA Samoyed University History of the Breed Questionnaire, and the recent use of a number of the SCA Foundation Greeting Cards in the SCA Judges' Education Power Point presentation.

All of this activity started with Rex and the developing research on his life, his contemporaries, and other important Samoyeds, breeders, and owners. The notes, storyline, and pictures on Rex of White Way were originally intended to be used in the docu-drama on Rex. The Rex docu-drama promotional DVD is already in production as I finalize this latest project—the book on Rex. It is as if Rex's spirit is still alive, compelling us all to tell his story!

I never considered myself a book author and was waiting for someone else to write the story on Rex. Michael told me to write down in ten pages or less what Rex was about. As time went on, the ten pages easily became 70 single-spaced pages, and that was not including the interview notes from Lloyd Van Sickle.

There is a "story-behind-the-story" in finally locating Lloyd in 2004. Some of us had thought that Lloyd had passed away in the 1970s. Others outside of sledding circles had never heard of him. Certainly a few stories had appeared in mushing magazines and Samoyed publications referencing Lloyd and Rex together, but no mention was ever made that Lloyd was still alive when I began pulling the Rex story together. In March 2004, after I finally found a one-year-old reference to Lloyd in a mushing "chat room," by searching for "Lloyd Van Sickle and Targhee Hounds" on my (frustrating) dial-up Internet connection, I was talking to Lloyd's son some 48 hours later!

I had placed a picture on my keyboard overnight of Rex in his harness that showed him after he set the "World Record" in Weight Pulling! It was taken after he won the title, "The Strongest Dog on the Planet" in 1954 at West Yellowstone, Montana.

REX, *The Blizzard King*: "**THE KEYBOARD**" **PICTURE!**
COURTESY MARDEE WARD-FANNING.

The next day I heard back from someone by e-mail who reported that he had just spent part of the evening with Lloyd down in Mt. Shasta, California. I remember telling Celinda: "Finding Lloyd is still alive is like coming across Amelia Earhart hanging on to a propeller shaft somewhere in the South Pacific!"

Just to be sure, the first thing I asked Steve Van Sickle (Lloyd's son) when I called by telephone was, "Is your dad still alive?" Steve responded, "He was about 30 minutes ago...when he went out to feed the Targhee Hounds."

When I finally had Lloyd on the phone, one of the first things I had to ask him was, "Could Rex really climb a tree?" Lloyd said that sometimes people say things for fun or for a reporter or for a publication, but he answered me that he had never actually asked Rex to climb a tree, so he didn't truly know if he could have done it or tried it.

The on-site interview, a few weeks after the initial phone call, was termed a "religious experience" by one of the parties attending, and Lloyd told one of the interviewers that he "never could get that close to a sled dog again after Rex passed away in 1957." Steve remarked to me after the interview that in all his years he had never seen his dad open up the way he did when talking about Rex in our 2004 interview.

LLOYD VAN SICKLE AND HIS SON STEVE DURING THE 2004 INTERVIEW.

Years later, my beloved Samoyed, Riley, won his "Best in Show" out of the "Veteran's Class" at the Samoyed Club of America National in Utah on October 15, 2011. Before we left the hotel for the show site, I showed Riley the glossy 8″ x 10″ picture of Rex in harness that Mardee Ward-Fanning, AKC judge, breeder, and author, had given me earlier that week for the Rex book and docu-drama. This was the same picture I had placed on the keyboard when I found Lloyd in 2004, only larger! I told Riley that he had a "double legacy" to live up to (his great sire, Ono, had won the National in 2000), and that he had to go out there and beat all the rest of the 320 Samoyeds entered because he was getting too old and this was his last National!

Riley looked at the picture of Rex, heard what I said, and seemed to make a connection. I think he understood. Riley rose to the occasion in grand fashion and is now in the record books for SCA…as he won his Best in Show at the once-a-year SCA National at the age of 10 years and 7 months.

Of course, he has Rex of White Way's blood in him!

ONO (ON THE LEFT) AND RILEY (ON THE RIGHT) WON THE SCA NATIONAL ELEVEN YEARS APART…ONO IN 2000 AND RILEY IN 2011. ALAN STEVENSON, SAMOYED BREEDER AND FORMER OWNER OF RILEY, IS STANDING BEHIND ONO. HANDLER, HEATHER STEVENSON KELLY, IS STANDING BEHIND RILEY.

YOUNG REX IN THE SNOW WITH A YOUNG LLOYD.
COURTESY GAIL SPIEKER.

REX—A SERIOUS, DEDICATED LEADER—DOING WHAT HE LOVED!

INTRODUCTION

Some dogs are "special"...called to greatness, honored for making a lasting difference in the lives of others. Rex of White Way was such a dog.

This is the story of a purebred Samoyed named Rex of White Way. Rex was bred by Agnes Mason and her daughter, Miss Aljean Mason of Sacramento, California and lived from 1946–1957. He was born on September 26, 1946 out of Ch. Herdsman's Faith by Ch. White Way of Kobe. A Samoyed is a double-coated Arctic breed that can be pure white, white and biscuit, cream, or all biscuit and is known as *a working dog.* The Samoyed currently ranks 70th in the United States in annual registrations out of more than 175 breeds recognized by the American Kennel Club.

Many stories and legends have developed over the past 50 years since Rex's passing. Some written statements concerning Rex can no longer be proven or disproven, but we can make certain generalized assumptions. Certainly Samoyed owners and exhibitors tended to glamorize Rex if he appeared in their own Samoyed's pedigree. One well known SCA breeder (Doris McLaughlin) relayed to me in 2003 that Agnes had once told her that Rex could play the piano. I don't know if he played Chopin, Liszt, or Rachmaninoff—just that he played the piano. We know it appears elsewhere in interviews with Aljean Mason that at least one other White Way Samoyed could play the piano.

From reliable sources, Rex's weight varied from 62 to 70 pounds. To be able to keep up with the Targhee Hounds, and actually lead them, Rex had to be fit and could not afford to pack extra poundage. Some stories are still in circulation reporting Rex's weight to be closer to 75 or 80 pounds. One eye witness to seeing Rex in harness thought that Rex stood 27 inches—yet the Samoyed Conformation Standard for males calls for 21 to 23½ inches with "an oversized or undersized Samoyed to be penalized according to the extent of the deviation."

Rex was exceptionally fit and had muscles built up from working very hard. His temperament was splendid, and it had to be in order to race—when he was less than two years old and with a four-year-old child (Sandy Van Sickle) as the driver, and later to lead 24 dogs in harness in San Mateo, California. Lloyd told us he once had Rex at lead with 60 dogs hitched behind him.

I thought it important in the book to provide background on Samoyeds, sledding, Agnes Mason, and Lloyd Van Sickle to help the reader appreciate how the historical Rex came to be. Many detailed stories and vignettes involving Rex fortunately survived over the last 55 years, which should help the reader appreciate Rex's life work more fully without the need to resort to invented (created) dialogue or scenes.

We tried to check airplane logs to see if Rex was ever listed as a passenger on small aircraft to verify that Rex was trained to parachute jump, but we couldn't verify this story. We do know it is a fact that several of the White Way Samoyeds were trained to parachute jump. It is probable that Rex was similarly trained, but we can offer no actual proof. At one point in the 2004 interview with Lloyd, he makes a single reference to Rex jumping from a plane but then contradicted that statement elsewhere when he stated Rex never jumped.

Lloyd told us that the other dogs in a team respected and didn't challenge Rex at lead because of his bearing, strength, and calmness. Seems like a good prescription for a successful political leader, football quarterback, or business executive, too.

Rex performed many arduous rescue missions (over 30) during his lifetime and fully exemplified the working characteristics of a Samoyed. There are other working breeds in addition to the purebred Samoyed. In today's specialized and fast paced world with instant communications, it is unlikely we will ever see or need another Rex who can excel in so many different venues. During his time, Rex created his own niche in mountain rescues, mail runs, and on movie sets. Not all of the rescues that were featured in the *Western Kennel World (WKW)* appear in surviving newspaper articles or, after five decades, appear in any recoverable written format.

"Rescue" was Rex's work assignment during the snow season and Lloyd was on call or made himself available when needed throughout an almost five-state area.

Rex's work on the mail run sled team over the 7,072 foot high Targhee Pass during the snow season is well documented. His contributions as lead sled dog on the stranded train *City of San Francisco* rescue in 1952 and the Truckee plane crash rescue of 1949 were captured in the

Sacramento Bee and the local Truckee, California newspaper. Rex set a world record in weight pulling for a purebred dog, won many sled races and weight pulls, worked for many seasons hauling Christmas trees up to 34 miles on each roundtrip, and appeared in regular "dog and pony" shows with Lloyd Van Sickle throughout most of his life.

Samoyed teams were often used on demonstration teams or in parades, with Rex at lead. He never became an American Kennel Club Champion of Record, yet he was the Top Male of all American born Samoyeds up through the mid-1970s in his contribution to the Samoyed gene pool through his breedings and his offspring. He unquestionably left his imprint on the breed!

As with the story of *Seabiscuit,* Rex's story has been waiting to be "uncovered" and pieced together. Agnes Mason, Rex's breeder, had thought before she died in 1970 that a movie should be made of Rex's life story. The Samoyed Club of America, through the American Kennel Club, identified and registered White Way Kennels in 2004 for kennel name protection along with four other U.S. Samoyed kennels. This was in recognition of the significant contributions of these kennels to furthering and promoting the breed.

One of the main reasons I became drawn to and subsequently involved with the breed in 1991 was because of the great contributions of the Polar Expeditions' Samoyed sled dog teams and of course Rex's achievements as captured in the Bob and Dolly Ward book. All of the Samoyeds that I have owned or co-owned can be traced back many times going through Rex of White Way. The vast majority of Samoyeds in the United States today, likewise, go back through Rex many, many times.

It seems there have been only a handful of movies made about dog shows. The recent *Best in Show* from the late 1990s comes easily to mind as well as much earlier (1930s) William Powell/Myrna Loy movies made during *The Thin Man* days. With some 40% of U.S. households today owning at least one dog, there would appear to be a great interest in a well-presented dog show story.

The purpose of writing the Rex story is to educate and inform the general public as well as the dog owning and dog showing public about Rex's heroic life. Those particularly familiar with the Samoyed breed or dog showing should appreciate the story of how the "ugly duckling" later became a star in breeding programs and truly excelled as a working canine—as one would expect from a member of a working breed.

As an "underdog," Rex worked his way to the top to prove he had the "right stuff" to merit consideration in national breeding programs. During Rex's time and especially today, purebreds who are not Conformation champions, never repeatedly make the top of the list for contributions to the breed's gene pool. Knowledgeable breeders don't usually go to extremes to breed to a non-champion grand-sire or great-grand sire either.

One of the main purposes of Conformation dog shows is to evaluate potential breeding stock. Arguably, this is the main purpose of dog shows. Rex lacked one major (3 points) or just a few points from obtaining his AKC Championship—which requires 15 points. (There is a difference of opinion on how many points he actually lacked.) His coat usually showed heavy wear and discoloration from the harness, which hindered him in the show ring when matched against the competition.

His competition in races and weight pulls for most of his lifetime was not other Samoyeds, as he was much faster and stronger; he really found his niche in races running with mixed breeds like Lloyd's Targhee Hounds. Was it the training, the breeding, his super strength and stamina, or luck?

What made Rex go?

Lloyd told us in the 2004 interview that "Rex was born to be a Leader" and he gave Rex the opportunity.

Above all, maybe it is as author Bob Ward remarked on one occasion:

"Rex was 5 pounds of bones and hair,
and the rest was all heart."

Rex had heart, high intelligence, speed, and world class strength. And that is why we have a story to tell!

**REX, IN THE SNOW IN IDAHO.
COURTESY KAY KETCHUM.**

"ON THE MOVE," ORIGINAL BLACK-AND-WHITE SKETCH BY PAM LANDERS.
PHOTOGRAPH BY NORMA PINKERT. COURTESY PAM LANDERS.

CHAPTER 1

THE BEGINNING OF SAMOYEDS

Our story of Rex of White Way probably had its beginnings many thousands of years ago in Asia. Wolves kept reappearing into human settlement areas because there was food there (garbage). Maybe this first wave of humans was pushing northward, possibly to escape an enemy and save their lives. Much later, over time, the wolf became "a dog" and was used for warmth, companionship, hunting, pulling sledges, guard duty, and herding among other duties. Jim Osborn, a respected Samoyed researcher and author, believes that the breed goes back at least 1,500 years.

A recent anthropological finding chronicled by Sandra Olsen, Ph.D., in 1998, documents a "crossroads" area in north central Kazakhstan dated 5,000 years ago. It unearthed the bones of canines (that were buried in small pits in or near houses) that most closely resemble in size and shape the Samoyed, but more robust. This does not mean to imply that these animals were Samoyeds or "early Samoyeds," as evidence was not available to ascertain coat, ears, or tail, for example. This "crossroads" was a well-traveled area for commerce and migration. Dr. Olsen, one of the three foremost authorities in the world on horse domestication, had traveled to Kazakhstan looking for horse bones. She found something else, too.

As stated in her Abstract:

> Based on osteometrics, the Botai dogs were comparable in size and morphology to the modern Samoyed breed. Patterning in the placement of canine remains in threshold and foundation pits is interpreted here as evidence of ritual behavior. Botai dogs possessed a close connection with houses that may reflect their roles as guardians.
>
> The practice of burying dogs in pits to the west of houses at Botai also appears from England to China in the subsequent

Bronze Age. According to later Indo-European and Indo-Iranian mythologies, dogs were the guardians of the gate to the Otherworld, which lay to the west. In death, dogs were also closely associated with horses, the only other known domesticated animal of the Botai. This spiritual association may be analogous to a more secular relationship concerned with hunting or herding.

During the summer of 2011, Dr. Susan Crockford co-authored a scientific report on the 33,000 year old potentially "incipient dog." Dr. Crockford reported that this was about the size of a modern Samoyed found in the Razboinichya Cave (Altai Mountains of southern Siberia). The well preserved remains of the dog-like canid was extraordinarily preserved including skull, mandibles (both sides), and teeth. In the report's conclusion, the author states, "The Razboinichya Cave specimen appears to be an incipient dog that did not give rise to late Glacial-early Holocene lineages and probably represents wolf domestication disrupted by the climatic and cultural changes associated with the LGM (Last Glacial Maximum). The two earliest incipient dogs from Western Europe (Goyet, Belgium) and Siberia (Razboinichya), separated by thousands of kilometers, show that domestication was multiregional, and thus had no single place of origin and subsequent spread."

Dr. Crockford emphasized in her discussions with me that the rough similarity in size and shape of the early dog-like canid from Siberia to a modern Samoyed does not imply any direct relationship—the analogy to a Samoyed was made for mental imaging purposes only. She also pointed out that a few more pre-Ice Age skulls have now been reported and as a consequence of the larger sample, it is no longer clear if these "dog-like" animals were indeed very early dogs or simply abnormally small wolves. Clearly, there is more work to be done understanding the relationship of pre-Ice Age wolves and humans!

However, the Crockford co-authored Report Summary by Jennifer Viegas on July 28, 2011, as it appeared on the Discovery News website, states that all modern dogs appear to be descended from ancestors that lived at the end of the Ice Age 17,000–14,000 years ago, and this still appears to be the case.

The dog is the oldest domesticated animal sharing our planet. This partnership has gone on for many thousands of years.

Rex is a fine example of how close a relationship can become between man and dog. Without Rex, Lloyd doesn't get his work finished in delivering the U.S. mail or supplies, rescuing humans, pulling large loads like planes, Christmas trees, boat dock piers for Donner Lake, transporting passengers, etc.

The dog has served with man as a companion and has helped him survive, explore, hunt, herd, enjoy free time, etc. But he didn't start off as a "dog," and how he came to be is an interesting story. All evidence to date suggests that all dogs in existence today have the wolf as their ancestor. Evolution from the wolf appears to have occurred at several places and during different times in history. It was believed for a long time that man tamed the wolf to create the domestic dog, but it now appears more likely that wolves who had a high stress tolerance came around continually to eat the left over scraps and garbage left behind. They stayed near the campsites for ready food, and bred with each other instead of rejoining their wolf ancestors. It was more a case of the wolf adapting and going through evolutionary changes than that man deliberately domesticated the wolf. Any "incipient dogs" that may have emerged before the last Ice Age appear to have died out during the cold period that followed, as people moved around more during the Ice Age.

Dr. Crockford reported in the March 2012 *Dog Fancy* magazine that "...the Ice Age-induced climate change may have forced people into a more nomadic—and less wolf attractive existence." But evolution from wolf to dog (*"Wolf to Woof"* as Dr. Crockford likes to say) occurred again to bring us the dog at a later time and place.

According to the same article in *Dog Fancy*, while domestic dogs do share some of the same behaviors with wolves, the domestication process brought about significant changes. Dr. Crockford continues "...when wolves became dogs, changes in size, shape, growth rate, physiology, and brain development led to behavioral changes."

It is reported that the Egyptians tried to domesticate almost every conceivable animal. The lion and tiger, for example, have not been domesticated even today. You don't want them in the house as pets as they are not reliable. The pig appears to have been the second animal to be domesticated and that is probably because, like the wolf, it is considered a scavenger. In order, domestication (per Dr. Crockford) was as follows: dog, pig, goat/sheep almost simultaneous, cow, horse, and then cat a few thousand years later! The cat has only been domesticated since about 3,000 B.C. Some may argue that cats are not fully domesticated, but I have a cat (Jimmi) who comes when called and follows my hand signals when I want her to move.

Dr. Crockford told me that some evidence suggests cats possibly were domesticated earlier (along the lines of goats/sheep, along with pigeons and mice) but that this is limited and perhaps not very well supported. (These would be outdoor cats and not "house" cats.) Dr. Crockford in her book, *Rhythms of Life, Thyroid Hormone and the Origin of Species*, presents the theory that thyroid hormone drives domestication and speciation. The stress tolerant animals who invaded human settlements became new species (in other words, "domesticated") because of the variable thyroid function among individuals within the ancestral species. The individuals who invaded ("colonized") human settlements were a particular subset of the animals in the ancestral population: only those individuals with a particular thyroid hormone metabolism were involved in the domestication process. This biological mechanism could set evolutionary changes in motion because thyroid hormone controls so many critical functions, including stress response, fetal and juvenile growth rates, reproduction, and brain function.

Once animals had changed biologically (become a new, "domesticated" species), humans could deliberately select individuals that suited them best.

Once dogs became a new species distinct from wolves, humans had both direct and indirect influences on which animals survived and bred. It could not have been an easy life for dogs but it was not easy for people either. However, almost certainly, only the dogs able to endure environmental challenges such as weather extremes as well as human demands would have survived through thousands of generations.

In modern times, knowledgeable breeders use only their best stock for producing offspring. One should always try to improve on the breed with each planned breeding. With a purebred dog, one knows what is behind the dam and sire and can predict with great accuracy what the new puppy, and later the adult dog, will look and act like as well as what health issues may be present or absent.

As the American Kennel Club (AKC) says in its *Online Breeder Classifieds* website: "The bonus of selecting a purebred dog is their predictability in size, coat, care requirements, and temperament." This is why knowledgeable Samoyed breeders wanted Rex in the pedigrees of the Samoyed puppies. They wanted to keep the ultimate working Samoyed genes going!

With this as background, the Samoyed, although we don't know its exact age, has been with mankind for a long period of time and is not generally considered a "modern" dog. Despite its attractive appearance and look of elegance, with its tail carried over the back, the Samoyed is a very hardy breed. It had to be "robust" to survive on the frozen tundra and in cold climates. Small lap dogs like Bichons and short-coated dogs like Daschunds, for example, could not have survived the rugged lifestyle.

THIS SAMOYED IS POSSIBLY WAITING FOR MORE SNOW TO SHOW THAT HE MIGHT HAVE WHAT IT TAKES TO TEAM UP WITH LLOYD AND REX ON SOME OF THEIR WINTER ADVENTURES IN AND AROUND TRUCKEE, CALIFORNIA. ONE HAS TO ASSUME HE GETS SOME HELP IN GOING UP THE NATION'S FIRST MECHANIZED SKI LIFT. HE LOOKS LIKE HE IS READY, THOUGH, TO COME DOWN UNDER HIS OWN POWER. COURTESY TRUCKEE DONNER HISTORICAL SOCIETY. THANKS ALSO TO THE TRUCKEE CHAMBER OF COMMERCE, AND TO FRANK ROSSBACK.

History

The name "Samoyed" was given by Earnest Kilburn-Scott for the Samoyed tribe of people. Earnest Kilburn-Scott, an accomplished engineer, and a professor later in the United States, helped procure "Samoyeds" for Polar Expeditions and later imported several dogs to his England home where he and his wife helped establish the breed.

The Samoyed tribe of people from the north of Russia and Siberia used the Samoyed to pull sledges, serve as a guard dog, and herd reindeer. By working in a pack, the Samoyed could frighten and contain even the great polar bear! One Samoyed may not bring down a bear on its own, but three would probably be more than a fair match. And because of his double coat, the Samoyed was probably used from early times to warm his master and family in cold weather.

Man harnessed the Samoyed's enthusiasm, adaptability for work in harsh climates, intelligence, and ability to understand him and made the Samoyed into a working partner. In return, the Samoyed received food, friendship, and was welcomed into the chums/tents at night as an ally.

"Greenland Scenery" porcelain plate
(Royal Copenhagen, Denmark).
Photograph by Noel Johnson. Courtesy Jim Cheskawich.

Over time, pure white, cream, all biscuit, or white and biscuit became the acceptable coat colors. (See the Official Standard for the Samoyed in *The Complete Dog Book of the American Kennel Club*.) The early Samoyed dogs were black as well as brown. Although many of today's Samoyeds are groomed to perfection, particularly the Samoyeds exhibited in the Conformation Show Ring, it may be hard to believe that the early Samoyed dogs were probably heavily matted in sections, with only the sun serving as a bleaching agent.

From the 2010 SCA/AKC approved handout flyer mailed by AKC to new puppy owners (See Appendix E): "Samoyeds know how to think for themselves and can get bored without a variety of activities and close relationships with people. They are a breed that may chase, run and bark due to their heritage. They are not a dog to be tied out in the backyard and forgotten! ... a Samoyed is a working dog and is happiest when he has a job, even if it is just bringing in the daily paper."

We can see with Rex that he would get bored from being kept in a hotel room by himself for a few hours because he would crash through windows to find something to do! Like Rex, all Samoyeds need space, exercise, and preferably a working function. The Samoyed is almost human in its intelligence and since man has worked with the Samoyed for many hundreds of years, it is not hard to understand why.

Lloyd and Rex spent a lot of time together, and just as a well trained horse can sense through telepathy when you want to pick up a trot, Rex and Lloyd had a similar connection in regard to what each was thinking.

THE POLAR EXPEDITIONS

The Polar Expeditions demonstrated the versatility and true working nature of the Samoyed. The contributions made by the Samoyeds are *unmatched* in the canine world. Samoyeds featured prominently in the Arctic and Antarctic Polar Expeditions of Abruzzi, Amundsen, Jackson-Harmsworth, Nansen, and Shackelton between 1870 and 1912. Dogs were procured from Siberia for the expeditions and were called "Samoyeds," as they came from the land where the Samoyede tribe lived. With the passing of time, the "e" was dropped from "Samoyede."

The draft animals proved more capable than ponies, horses, oxen, or mules in the Arctic and Antarctic and, on a per weight basis, did not consume as much food and could travel longer distances before tiring.

ROYAL CONNECTIONS

A beautiful breed, the Samoyed appeared in the courts of Czar Alexander III of Russia and Queen Alexandra of England over a century ago. They were made pets because of their great beauty, adaptability, and intelligence.

The History Channel on television in the United States has shown movie pictures of Samoyeds driven in early automobiles in London over a century ago. Several still photos capture the Samoyed in official family photos of the Russian Royal Family.

THE SMIRNOFFS AND SAMOYEDS

It has been reported that the head of the Smirnoff Vodka Distillery and family used a team of Samoyeds to travel quickly across Siberia to flee the Russian Revolution of 1917. Mr. Smirnoff reestablished his business in Constantinople/Istanbul, and also the family business was eventually set up in the United States.

RUSSIAN CERAMIC. PHOTOGRAPH BY NOEL JOHNSON.
COURTESY JIM AND CELINDA CHESKAWICH.

THE FIRST IMPORTS TO THE UNITED STATES

The first Samoyed registered with The American Kennel Club in the United States, Russian Champion Moustan of Argenteau, came from St. Petersburg, Russia from Grand Duke Nicholas, a brother of the Czar. Survivors and descendants of the Polar Expedition sledge teams were bred in England for their beauty as well as their working attributes.

It was around this time that black and brown were eliminated from breeding pools, although pictures remain of the Samoyed, Ch. Peter the Great, and his offspring (some were black) who competed successfully in the Conformation Ring in England.

Almost all Samoyeds living today in the United States can be traced back to 12 key dogs that were used in early breeding programs in England. One of the truly great sires in the breed was English Champion Kara Sea, who figured prominently in many breeding programs on both sides of the Atlantic Ocean.

In the sport of purebred dogs, "**Ch.**" means a dog (**D-male**) or bitch (**B-female**) has earned 15 championship points, including two majors, to be awarded the **prefix of "Champion"** (**Ch.**) before its registered name. When referring to offspring, the "**sire**" is the father of the canine and the "**dam**" is the mother.

**ALJEAN MASON OF WHITE WAY KENNELS
WITH CH. WHITE WAY OF KOBE.**

THE MOST IMPORTANT
EARLY BRITISH IMPORTS TO THE U.S.

a. Ch. Siberian Nansen of Farningham of Snowland (D)

b. Ch. Zahrina of Norka (B)

c. Silver Spark of the Arctic (D)

d. Ch. Storm Cloud (D)

e. **Ch. White Way of Kobe (D) (Rex's sire)**

f. Morina of Taimir (B)

g. Am/Eng Ch. Tiger Boy of Norka (D)

h. Ch. Tobolsk (D)

i. Ch. Snow Frost of the Arctic (D)

j. Ch. Donerna's Barin (D)

NOTE: There have been many important Samoyed kennels and breeders in the United States during the establishment of the breed in the United States in the first half of the 20th century. They include: Donerna, Yurak, Obi, Norka, Laika, and Park-Cliffe. Two kennels stand out above all the others because of their overall contribution to the breed: Snowland Kennels and White Way Kennels. Since 2004, the American Kennel Club and the Samoyed Club of America protect both kennel names.

COURTESY JIM OSBORN.

SNOWLAND KENNELS AND HELEN HARRIS

Mrs. Helen Harris of Merion, Pennsylvania obtained a son of Ch. Kara Sea's (Ch. Siberian Nansen of Farningham of Snowland) in the 1930s and used him to establish her Snowland Kennels in the United States. Nansen is the top foreign born Samoyed in terms of his contribution to the gene pool (from Jim Osborn, Samoyed historian, statistician, writer, engineer).

Early in the 1930s, Mrs. Harris had traveled to Europe with her daughter, Faith, and returned with her first Samoyed, Pedlar of the Arctic, who was procured as a pet for Faith. Mrs. Harris contributed greatly to the establishment of the breed in the United States and her Samoyeds figured prominently in the start up of many long-standing and successful kennels, including that of Agnes Mason and her White Way Kennels in Sacramento, California.

PAINTING OF "CH. ICE CRYSTAL OF THE ARCTIC" BY FAITH HARRIS CHILD,
DAUGHTER OF HELEN HARRIS.
PHOTOGRAPH BY NOEL JOHNSON.
COURTESY JIM CHESKAWICH.

Mrs. Harris had a now famous "N" litter (Champions Nadya, Norna, Nim, Nianya, and Nikita) by Siberian Nansen out of Vida of Snowland that really propelled the breed forward in the U.S.

Mrs. Harris also believed in working her Samoyeds in harness hitched to a sled, serving as evidence of the working capabilities of the breed. She had a large kennel, which was common for the day, along with a kennel manager.

WHITE WAY KENNELS AND AGNES MASON

From all reports available, Agnes Mason was a very hard working business woman who carried over this trait to managing her White Way Samoyed Kennels. She was married to A. E. Mason, and they had three children, including a daughter, Aljean Mason, who was born in 1927 and who played an active role in the running of the kennel and in showing the dogs.

Prior to getting involved with Samoyeds, the Masons had Chows imported from China. They were remembered as good specimens, but were never shown. Agnes Mason's first Samoyed, Czar Nicholas Lebanov, was purchased in 1935 from M. D. McDowell of Oakland, California, whom she first met at a California State Fair dog show. He was purchased for sled work and not principally to be shown.

Aljean, who was about eight-years-old at the time, hooked him up to a wagon, and rode him around the neighborhood. This was her "introduction" to driving a dog. Mr. A. E. Mason put wheels on the sled, which belonged to Agnes Mason's father and had been used in Alaska. When the family moved into the countryside near Sacramento, they started raising Sams, finishing their first male out of the litter. (This was Petrof Lebanov, a son of Czar Nicholas Lebanov and Dascha of Laika, a bitch from back east.)

ALJEAN MASON AND CZAR NICHOLAS.

**JUDGE DUPON AND AGNES MASON WITH: (LEFT TO RIGHT)
CH. TROOPERINE OF WHITE WAY, REX OF WHITE WAY, WHITE WAY'S JACKO,
CH. WHITE WAY SILVER STREAK.**

Agnes Mason obtained Ch. Nianya of Snowland in 1938 from Helen Harris out of the famous "N" litter of Ch. Siberian Nansen of Farningham of Snowland and Vida of Snowland. Through carefully planned acquisitions and breedings from Arctic (England), Kobe (England), Snowland, and Laika Kennels, Mrs. Mason combined several strong lines in developing her foundation stock.

Prior to Rex of White Way's arrival in 1946 out of her own Ch. Herdsman's Faith (born on September 30, 1940) and Ch. White Way of Kobe (born on March 28, 1938), Mrs. Mason had developed a reputation as an outstanding breeder and Conformation Show exhibitor in addition to working her Samoyeds in harness.

The name "White Way" came from Ch. White Way of Kobe who was imported from England.

**CH. HERDSMAN'S FAITH,
REX'S DAM.**

THE MOST IMPORTANT
EARLY AMERICAN BRED DOGS

1. Vida of Snowland (B)

2. **Ch. Herdsman's Faith (B) (Rex's dam)**

3. Ch. Nianya of Snowland (B)

4. **Rex of White Way (D)**

5. Cleo (B)

6. White Frost's Tybo (D)

7. Nikita of Snowland (D)

8. Ch. Starchak (D)

9. Ch. Omak (D)

10. Ch. Lucky Labon Nahum (D)

11. Ch. Stormy Weather of Betty Blue (D)

12. Soldier Frosty of Rimini (D)
    (See following: "1948 Parachuting Samoyeds")

13. Ch. Petrof Lebanof (D)

14. Sooltan (D

15. Ch. Silver Star of White Way (B)

16. Dascha of Laika (B)

17. Mitzi-Aura Laska (B)

18. Kikmik of Oceanside (D)

19. Sonolad of The Valley (D)

20. Niarivik of Inara (B)

COURTESY JIM OSBORN.

World War II:
1948 Parachuting Samoyeds

Several of Mrs. Mason's Samoyeds were trained, with the assistance of Lewis Price, to parachute from small aircraft to help out in rescue operations. Per Alta Van Sickle (trainer Lloyd Van Sickle's wife), Lewis Price was a friend of Lloyd's and a fellow musher. Mrs. Mason and Lloyd thought it was a good publicity vehicle and served to show how Samoyeds could be used in rescue missions. The sled was dropped first with parachute attached; then the dogs were dropped, one by one, with parachutes attached; then Lewis Price parachuted down and with the assistance of a musher's helper, gathered up the dogs, hooked them to a sled, and drove them, in one instance, to a nearby starting line where he then entered the Freight Race.

Lewis Price was just out of the U.S. Army as a parachutist. Being trained to parachute further demonstrates the adaptability and trainability of the Samoyed. However, Mrs. Mason did not continue to parachute her dogs for very long, due to the criticism from membership of the Samoyed Club of America (SCA).

In 1942, Agnes volunteered her Samoyeds for service in the U.S. Army. One of Mrs. Mason's Samoyeds, Soldier Frosty of Rimini (owned by Miss Barbara Stewart of California) was inducted into the K-9 Corps of the U.S. Army, helped in the war effort, and received a Good Conduct Medal and a Victory Medal after World War II! Soldier Frosty was discharged on May 19, 1944. Soldier Frosty served on Attu, Iceland, and Greenland as lead dog of a team used to take supplies in to fliers downed in icy terrain. He was made a Colonel in the Reserve Corps. (From *The Complete Pedigree Book of American Champion Samoyeds Volume One* and the Gertrude Adams' files.)

Had Rex of White Way never lived, Mrs. Mason's contribution to the development of the Samoyed breed would still have been considered enormous.

Soldier Frosty served his country for one year and received an Honorable Discharge (left).

Courtesy of Pat deBack

WORLD WAR II U. S. ARMY MEDAL WINNER,
COL. SOLDIER FROSTY OF RIMINI.

The story was continued later in the April 1952 *Western Kennel World (WKN)* magazine:

> "Parachuting of the Sacramento Samoyeds to the race track was in line," Mrs. Mason stated (in an item for *Alta Pet News* in March 1948), "with the Army's experimentation in developing rescue crews of this type for use in the Arctic." The experience gained by the team in rescue work came in good use in a recent rescue event—when Rex the lead dog and one of his pals left the San Francisco show where they had gained honors for themselves to be flown to Truckee, to be met by Lloyd Van Sickle, thence to go by sled to take part in rescuing the couple marooned in a snow blanketed house in the snowbound Sierras.
>
> Because of the success of this undertaking, Mrs. Mason has decided to leave the trained team with Lloyd Van Sickle during the pressing need for rescue work. The latter is difficult at best—and to use a green team would make matters worse. This change from life as successful show dogs to actual rescue work is another proof of the versatility of the Samoyed—and further proves there is no need of dividing our breed into two types as some recommend. Any Sam can be trained to meet any demand put upon it, is the opinion of those who really know our breed.

Thus Rex ended up back with Lloyd in the mountains, so he could be more accessible for rescue work.

SAMOYEDS TODAY

Samoyeds, lovingly called "Sams" or "Sammys" by their owners and fans, are enjoyed today for their beauty, companionship, intelligence, and working versatility. As Mardee Ward-Fanning said in her interview: "This is a natural breed and not man-made, and excels as a service and companion dog. We shouldn't alter the breed, as it has been this way for many years."

As a working dog, Samoyeds are used to herd sheep, ducks, and cattle and can be found in sledding races and weight pulls held throughout the U.S. However, there aren't as many Samoyeds sledding compared to half a century ago. Owners regularly enjoy working their Samoyeds in backpacking, *skijoring*, scootering, and hiking in addition to the AKC sponsored obedience and agility events. Samoyeds also swim and hunt birds. For others, AKC Conformation Shows provide an opportunity to show their dogs in competition against other Samoyeds and other breeds.

Samoyeds are not noted for their great speed as compared to the Siberian Huskies or Alaskan Huskies or some of the mixed racing breeds found in races such as the Iditarod. Samoyeds are considered faster than Malamutes, who are known as the heavy pulling freight breed, but are not as fast as the Siberian Huskies.

The heart and loyalty of the Samoyed make it an exceptional dog, and drivers of Samoyed teams will not tolerate disparaging comparisons with any other dog team. Samoyeds are more concerned personally with their human contacts and leaders and have a more pronounced desire to please. The Samoyed is somewhat more apt to stand up to pressure than is the typical Arctic breed and they often excel under less than perfect conditions, where other dogs may lose heart. Samoyeds have a native stubbornness and strong will, which once turned to the driver's advantage, will keep them working consistently and hard.

Samoyeds are generally in the middle of the pack, speed wise, among the Arctic breeds. An all-Samoyed team usually doesn't beat a mixed breed team of 8–12 dogs (of Labrador, Malamute, Greenland, and Hound crosses) in long distance races. There are exceptions and some current well trained and conditioned Samoyed teams of 2, 4, and 6 dogs are consistently winning races today against all competition.

There are also well-trained Samoyed teams of 8–12 dogs that currently place well in long races against all competition. Targhee Hounds are a mixed breed created by Lloyd Van Sickle, and Rex was fast enough to lead Lloyd's hound teams while in his prime.

The Samoyed is considered by many to be a "high maintenance" breed because of its double coat necessitating the need for a regular weekly combing schedule, the shedding, the barking and digging, their escapist tendencies, and the need for constant exercise to ward off boredom and possible destructive chewing problems. The Samoyed is not a breed for everyone to consider owning. Many Samoyeds, unfortunately, end up in a rescue situation because the owners cannot take proper care of their Samoyed. The puppy with "Christmas on its face" can be a difficult adult to live with—in the wrong owner's hands.

Today's popularity of the Samoyed among dog breeds places it in the middle (#70) of all AKC recognized breeds, which is roughly where it has been for the past two decades. And today, just as from its beginnings, Samoyeds and their owners are deeply bonded.

STAINED-GLASS SAMOYED LAMP BY SAL LAWRENCE, M.D., MOSCOW, PA.
PHOTOGRAPH BY NOEL JOHNSON.
COURTESY JIM CHESKAWICH.

RUSSIAN WOODCARVING.
PHOTOGRAPH BY NOEL JOHNSON. COURTESY JIM CHESKAWICH.

GREG AND JULIA KETCHUM, CIRCA 1959, WITH KING PIN, A REX DESCENDANT.
COURTESY KAY KETCHUM.

27

REX LACKED ONE MAJOR (3 POINTS), OR JUST A FEW POINTS, FROM OBTAINING HIS AKC "CHAMPIONSHIP"—WHICH REQUIRES 15 POINTS. ALJEAN MASON STATED (IN A *SAMOYED QUARTERLY* INTERVIEW) THAT REX NEVER FINISHED HIS CHAMPIONSHIP, BUT DID HAVE BOTH MAJORS AND NEEDED TWO OR THREE MORE POINTS TO FINISH. BUT HE WAS ALWAYS TOO BUSY DOG-MUSHING SOMEWHERE TO BE BOTHERED WITH THE DOG SHOWS.

OTHER REPORTS FROM OTHER SOURCES SHOW REX WITH 9-TO-13 POINTS AND ONE MAJOR. AT THE SUN MAID KENNEL SHOW IN 1952, REX GOT A RESERVE TO A FOUR POINT MAJOR. IF HE HAD WON WINNER'S DOG ON THIS DATE, REX WOULD NOW HAVE A "CH." BY HIS NAME IN THE PEDIGREE LISTINGS, AND WE WOULD BE WRITING ABOUT "CHAMPION REX OF WHITE WAY—*THE BLIZZARD KING*."

CHAPTER 2

THE REX STORY
WHERE IT ALL BEGAN:
WHITE WAY KENNELS AND
AGNES MASON—REX'S BREEDER

As Gertrude Adams (author of the current *Samoyed Illustrated Standard,* Samoyed historian, and architectural engineer) remarked in her collection of historical materials on Samoyeds, "...writing the history of Mrs. Agnes Mason and her famous White Way Kennels so many years after she has left us would require a book, rather than a chapter, to do her justice."

Mary Agnes Bauer Mason was born in Missouri in 1890 and spent her early life in Nome, Alaska, where she learned firsthand the importance of a sled dog as the primary means of transportation. She often made sled trips as far as 50 miles from Nome. Agnes was the daughter of an Alaskan gold miner. Mrs. Mason remarked in later years (in her 1952 Letter of Appreciation to SCA Members) that she was certain that one lead dog her father used was a Sam.

Agnes moved to California in 1912 and married Mr. A. E. Mason, who was from North Dakota. Agnes and her husband had three children: Commander Frank Mason was in the Navy, Mrs. Gertrude Glenn, and Aljean Mason Larson.

In 1915 Agnes started a direct mail auto registration in California, which has now grown into the current California Department of Motor Vehicles system. She also became the *first woman* in the State Legislature in California. Mr. A. E. Mason had a business, "Mason List and Advertising," which was a direct mail advertising business, which searched motor vehicle records. The businesses were eventually combined. Mr. Mason, who was in poor health, died in 1952 unexpectedly, and Agnes passed away in 1970. Agnes lived 58 years in California.

The Property

The property in the Sacramento countryside had a big two-story barn on it that had been used to house Clydesdales; the Masons made it into a kennel. They put wire gates in the front of the stalls and placed two dogs to a compartment at night. The barn had cement floors, except for the tie stalls, which had wooden floors. The females in heat were kept in the box stalls, because they were "dog proof (except maybe until Rex came along). In the mornings all the dogs were turned loose in the yard and they ran together. There were a couple of males that wanted to fight so they were kept on opposite sides. The Masons used to have Halloween parties and dances upstairs because it had such a slick floor, which may have been from the former days of hauling the hay across it, which made it appear like glass.

Czar Nicholas was great for opening gates, which opened inwards to the dogs. Nicholas learned how to get his teeth into the wire and jiggle it until the latch on the outside would bounce up. Then he would back up, holding the latch in his teeth, thereby letting all the dogs out of the kennel. The Mason dogs would run out and terrorize the neighborhood, costing chickens a few times and a swan once. Nick learned to turn doorknobs, sing, play on the piano, and howl. He did a lot of commercials and "singing" on the radio.

The Early Days

The first trainer for breaking the dogs to sled was Bill Thompson from Sunnyvale, California. The Masons did some obedience work starting with Czar Nicholas. He became an AKC Champion in the Conformation Ring. With just their own dogs, they had a dog team.

The breedings developed and Mrs. Mason became interested in proving that sled dogs could be work dogs and show dogs at the same time. That was her main goal, according to Aljean Mason.

Aljean also related that they were in three dog shows before someone tipped them off on how to enter. All Aljean wanted was to enter a class that offered a trophy. Any kid of that age only wants a trophy!

Early on, Agnes and Aljean got involved in doing parades, a lot of charity work, publicity, creating dog races, doing a lot of children's events for orphanages, Christmas shows, Easter Seal shows, the Hollywood Christmas parade, working at Treasure Island in San Francisco, and they showed a lot of dogs. At age 11, Aljean drove the Mason Team in their first race on Treasure Island during the World's Fair. Mr. Mason helped on many of these occasions. One Christmas, according to Agnes' 1952 Letter of Appreciation addressed to the Samoyed Club of America, "We carried about every Santa Claus in Sacramento—to churches, schools, street parades, club luncheons, the Governor's party, and Nick even modeled at a fashion show."

Aljean did most of the handling at the dog shows except when they had more than one or two. In some shows they had as many as twelve or fifteen dogs entered, and that is when entries were $3 a head. At some of the shows where they used the dogs for parade work, someone else sponsored the dog team so they didn't have to pay the entry fee for that many dogs. Aljean said they mainly did a lot of sled work. Lloyd Van Sickle was the trainer and he lived with his family at the Mason's. In the beginning, it was just Lloyd and Alta Van Sickle working for the Masons.

Mason dog team exhibited for "Dogs in Defense" about 1942. Far left: Aljean Mason, Center: Lloyd Van Sickle, driver. On his left in dark suit, Alta Van Sickle

Courtesy of Sandra Flettner

**FROM *THE SAVVY SAMOYED*, PAT HILL GOODRICH.
WITH PERMISSION.**

Training Tips

According to Aljean, there are a lot of techniques when training dogs. "They have to learn to stay in line, pull ahead instead of back. If I were breaking in a new dog, I would use two experienced dogs at wheel, the new dog at point, with another good dog next to it, and then an experienced lead dog. They would keep the new dog straightened out. You have to have a good lead dog to keep the line tight, because if the others get their feet over, you are in trouble. When they would get their feet over it, the line would get them in the groin and they'd learn real fast! You have brakes on the sled, and so you have control from the back; but you had to know what you were doing.

"We taught them to *gee* (Go right) and *haw* (Go left), and *Come around, gee* which meant to make a reverse. And *whoa* is Whoa! (Laughter). All you had to do was say, *Let's go!* and they were gone! That first lunge was really something."

Lloyd Van Sickle (not seen), with Leader Rex of White Way—at Donner Summit.

White Way Kennels'
Excellent Breeding System

The breedings kept improving and some of the best dogs were sold to Alaska. Agnes always bred with temperament in mind. Agnes usually placed her best dogs and left Aljean to finish what was left over. According to Aljean, "My mother was a terrible dog show handler; not that she couldn't get the dog squared up alright, but she just didn't like getting in the ring and running around ..." Aljean remarked in the *Samoyed Quarterly* that it seems they never kept the best dogs.

"Many breeders seem to keep the best," said Aljean, "but we always felt we were selling our best stock, and that a reputation is built on what you sell, not on what you keep. You don't want to send your culls out to people who want to breed or show. That will come back and haunt you. That is why my mother's reputation was what it was; she was not a dishonest person and she wasn't one to camouflage or cover anything up. That just wasn't her style. The litters were pretty uniform and similar in substance and quality. Good show dogs sold for $75 to $125 in the 1950s and 60s. Those sent to Alaska went for $150 to $200. The bitches were always cheaper than the males as there was more demand for males in those days and many people don't want to bother going through the heat cycle, and if you have a show dog, you wouldn't want to spay it."

Aljean also stated: "Our stock won on its own merit. There were no payoffs, or dinners, or anything like that. If we used a handler, he just sent us his bill and we paid it. We usually only had a handler for the Breed judging, never for Group judging. I did that. If we knew a judge was partial to handlers, we would use one for the Breed, but I always gave the handler the best dog too! Then if he would win, I would take the dog in the Group. I had a couple of handlers who were very unhappy I did that. I realize they get more money, and more publicity, but I felt the DOG won it."

By studying the pedigrees, Agnes worked out most of the breedings by herself. Most of the breedings were line breedings as she knew the background, what the dogs were like, the stock, and good qualities and bad qualities. By combining these, the Masons had a better tendency to improve the bloodline and to get the dog nearest to the standard. They had firsthand knowledge, which can only come from a large kennel operation. They bred to outside bitches but were very selective. And, as Aljean also said: "They all had to meet Mother's Specifications!"

SOME OF AGNES MASON'S BEST: CH. HERDSMAN'S FAITH, REX'S DAM, IS SECOND FROM THE LEFT.

Christmas Greetings from
The WHITE WAY Samoyeds

Mrs. A. E. Mason and Aljean Mason Larson
Rte 6, Box 3483 — Sacramento, California
Every Sam Shown Has Worked in the Sled Team

Aljean also said, "If you breed to something that is not worthy of the breed, that doesn't improve the breed, it tears it down. Some dogs have faults and you have to breed them out and in order to do it you have to sell the puppies that weren't good as pet stock with no papers. Then you go from there."

BOTH ALJEAN AND AGNES ENJOYED THE DOGS!

Aljean helped with the breedings, and sometimes had input into who should be bred, but mainly she handled the dogs at the shows and played with them. Once she got started with her breeding program, it was very seldom that Agnes bred to an outside dog. Aljean referred to herself as "head pooper-scooper, dog musher, handler, and spoiled brat!" Mostly the shows were in California and Nevada. Aljean also helped settle dogs into the teams assisting first Bill Thompson and later Lloyd Van Sickle. Lloyd, of course, performed a lot of the driving work because the Sams were on the road constantly. Aljean later worked and also showed horses, but somehow still had time to be involved with the dog shows.

AGNES AND ALJEAN MASON ENJOYING A "WHITE" CHRISTMAS!

MASON SLED TEAM DINES AT THE HOTEL SENATOR IN SACRAMENTO, CALIFORNIA.
LEFT TO RIGHT: CLEO, CH. DASHNICK'S SAM, CH. PETROF LEBANOF, SILVER SPARK
OF THE ARCTIC, CH. WHITE WAY OF KOBE, WHITE PHANTOM OF THE ARCTIC.

AGNES MASON'S LEGACY

Over time, Agnes Mason became active in Samoyed clubs, becoming (in 1940) the first president of the Pacific Coast Samoyed Club. Later, when the Pacific Coast group was accepted by the Samoyed Club of America as a Division, Agnes was voted as the vice president. In 1947 she became president of the Samoyed Club of America. She helped rewrite the breed standard, which is now our present standard.

Aljean never belonged to the Samoyed Club of America nor the Pacific Coast Samoyed Club, and she went to a few of the meetings and to the dinners only because she was already there at the dog shows and the meetings were held in connection with them. She left all of the "politicking" up to her mother. Aljean knew of the politics at the shows, knew who the handlers were that you needed for certain judges, and she knew that certain judges liked certain dogs. She did a lot of the selecting of the dogs to be shown, who was shown and when.

Sometimes there were a string of dogs shown and they would go regardless. "They would help make points, too, if you have a dog you are trying to finish. You put in a couple extras to make points and hope you are the lucky one to win." Aljean became a very good handler.

Aljean thought that her mother liked Samoyeds over the Siberians or Malamutes because of the temperament. In the old days, the Siberians and Malamutes were pretty tough dogs. Her experience with them was in Alaska and it was a rough life up there. She was looking for a companion for Aljean, which primarily influenced her decision to get a Samoyed. The dogs were fed in the kennel in groups so they had to get along, with the only exception being a couple of personality clashes among a few males who didn't like each other. The dogs ordinarily didn't fight or growl in the kennel.

Aljean estimated in the *Samoyed Quarterly* that they had 30-35 litters. (As an aside, Gertrude Adams accounted for 56 litters based on her own review of the Agnes Mason records.) At least 25 were champions of those they kept. Others finished who were placed, but are not included in the figure of 25. The litters ranged from 4 to 9 and on average, 2 or 3 out of each litter finished their championship. One time Aljean remembered having 36 dogs in the kennel with some being puppies (younger than 6 months of age). Aljean did not remember having any litter without at least one champion. After A. E. Mason's death in 1952, the dog showing activities slowed down, but some of the dogs were shown as late as 1961.

According to Gertrude Adams, while doing all of the Pacific Coast Division and Samoyed Club of America work and taking care of Samoyeds, Agnes had a great place to relax. She relates that the Masons had a cabin on the Russian River near a grove of redwoods and Guerneville. It was a wonderful place for the dogs to run and go swimming. With the Wards and a few of their dogs, the Adams visited them one summer and had a fun time and a good rest—no Club work that time!

The Masons provided foundation stock for many who started with White Way Samoyeds or provided Samoyeds that became critical components of other breeding programs. Leona Powell Pederson, Bob and Dolly Ward, Gertrude and Ed Adams, Chuck and Gene Burr, Whitecliff Samoyeds, and the Bristols all obtained key Samoyeds from the Masons.

Also according to the Gertrude Adams' files, in addition to all of their other duties, Agnes and Aljean attended a lot of dog shows. From the records Agnes provided Gertrude, she started showing seriously in 1940—although she had gone to several shows before that. In all, the list Gertrude made showed a total of 146 shows—the last being in 1958. (Note: Aljean said in the *SQ* interview that they showed in 1961.)

Agnes Mason passed away December 1970.

Mrs. Mason's famous Samoyed dog team, California State Fair, Sacramento, 1941.

Photo used on a calendar she had made and sent to friends with season's greetings at Christmas.

Courtesy of Pat deBack

FROM *THE SAVVY SAMOYED,* PAT HILL GOODRICH.
WITH PERMISSION.

**BACK OF THIS PHOTO IS
STAMPED WITH:**

Mason Samoyed Kennels
Mr. & Mrs. A. E. Mason
Rt. 7 Box 3483
Sacramento, Calif.

TYPEWRITTEN IS:

Mason's Famous
Samoyed Dog Team
Driver Lloyd Van Sickle,
noted musher.
This team is entered in
the Sierra Dog Derby
Races March 5th & 6th at
Truckee, Calif.

THE IMPACT OF AGNES AND WHITE WAY KENNELS ON THE SAMOYED WORLD
WAS PROFOUND—AS DEPICTED BY THIS GROUPING OF PHOTOS.
COURTESY KAY KETCHUM.

BEST BUDDIES, LLOYD AND REX.

CHAPTER 3

LLOYD VAN SICKLE
REX'S TRAINER

According to the *Sprague River (SR)*, Oregon newspaper (2004), Lloyd (also known just as "Van") was born in 1918 in Wilford, Idaho. At the age of 15, he won the American Dog Derby when he passed himself off as a 16-year-old. He probably could have won the Derby earlier, but he didn't look old enough to enter.

When he was 16 years old, in 1934, he started working with sled dogs by hauling railroad ties in Montana. There wasn't any other way to get ties and supplies in to the workers building tracks in the winter after the train stopped running. Lloyd also carried mail six days a week from Max Pond Lodge to West Yellowstone, a distance of 28 miles one way. He made a round trip each night because he could rely on the snow being frozen hard enough to run a dog sled. During the day it was liable to be too soft and he would be in danger of breaking through.

Lloyd lived early on with the Masons in California and afterwards lived in Idaho, traveling back and forth. According to the *SR* 2004 newspaper article on Lloyd, he went to work in the mid-1940s for Mrs. Mason's White Way Kennels as a dog trainer, while still hauling mail in the winter.

Sometimes Agnes Mason sent the dogs to Lloyd in Idaho to grow some coat and then she would take them back to the heat of Sacramento and put them in the show ring. Lloyd said the first Samoyed he got started for Agnes was Chattigan. Agnes and Lloyd were the first ones to get the sled dog races started up at Truckee, California again. Then they became annual events. Lloyd eventually moved to Truckee, which is how he became so involved later on as a point of contact for the rescues.

From *SR:*

[Lloyd] won the American Dog Derby 11 times. He ran for 6 years, doing 12 races a year and never lost a race, well into the 1960s. Van and his son Steve are the only father and son teams to win the Derby. Van was the first man from the lower 48 states to go up to (Fairbanks) Alaska and win a sled dog race in 1955.

When he was interviewed by me for the Rex story, at the age of 86, Lloyd was training his Targhee Hounds for an upcoming Iditarod! According to Steve, he still wanted to take dogs up to the snow country along the Teton Peaks in Idaho right up until his passing away from double pneumonia at the age of 88. "It is hard to keep a good man down," as the saying goes. Lloyd had to be in superb physical condition all of his life to keep up with the dogs.

From *SR:*

He ran pack mules for 22 years down in California in the Truckee Forest and in the Willamette National Forest for over 20 years. He packed supplies and tools back in for firefighting operations. This was in wilderness areas where there were no roads. He is in the "U.S. Postal Hauler's Hall of Fame" in Washington, DC. Pictures of Van and his dog team are in the museum. He bought land in Sprague River and lived there up until his death in December 2006.

THE HILLTOP LODGE

At one time Lloyd owned all five cabins behind the Hilltop Lodge in Truckee, California. Lloyd and his family lived in the middle cabin, or third from the south. Often the dogs were tied up or fenced in and Rex was the one to more often be loose. It is very likely that Rex got used to going in and out of the Hilltop Lodge as if he owned the place.

Once Lloyd was asked to tend the bar at the Hilltop Lodge while the manager went into town on some business. When the manager returned after several hours, he noticed there were no tips in the tip jar. After checking the cash register and finding that there was only the money he had left when he went to town, he asked Lloyd where the money was from the last few hours of business. Lloyd responded, "You didn't tell me to charge anyone!"

LLOYD, ALTA, REX, AND THE TEAM AT THE HILLTOP LODGE.
COURTESY CAROL CHITTUM.

THE OLD HILLTOP LODGE. COURTESY MARK MCLAUGHLIN.

According to Steve, Lloyd was of Dutch, Irish, English, and French-Canadian ancestry. He had a special way to talk and work with dogs that enabled him to get inside of their heads. He was always busy and a person who always needed something to do. Lloyd was working and training the dogs right up to the very end. In the old days, Lloyd liked his Copenhagen Snuff and an occasional Lucky Lager or a sip of Jack Daniels or Johnny Walker Black Label. His musical tastes ran from Patsy Cline, Jim Reeves, and Hank Williams to Lawrence Welk.

Lloyd "invented" the Targhee Hounds sometime probably in the 1940s when he crossed Irish Setters, Stag Hounds, and Grey Hounds for speed and stamina. The result was fast sprint dogs!

Lloyd named the dogs "Targhee Hounds," probably after his old stomping grounds in the Targhee Pass between Ashton and West Yellowstone, Idaho. It was reported that Lloyd had a good eye for a dog although he didn't commonly talk about "turn of stifle" or "overangulation," for example, which breeders refer to today when critiquing breeding stock. It was said that Lloyd believed he could put any dog in harness and make him work. He knew how far to push a dog and when to back off. It was reported that to Lloyd a good dog had to be a big dog.

And Rex lived up to that in every regard! As author and breeder Mel Fishback remarked, "Rex grew to be a giant among Samoyeds."

LLOYD VAN SICKLE'S FAMOUS TARGHEE HOUNDS, WITH REX.

HOW LLOYD DID "BUSINESS"

In the May 2008 interview, Steve told us a story of a "claiming race" in the 1950s or 1960s where another driver claimed all of Lloyd's team as his own for a particular race. Lloyd had to go around and borrow a dog "here and there" to make a team to run the race. Lloyd ended up beating his *own* team that particular race day with borrowed dogs! Steve said that his dad's team had been unbeaten for a long time, until Lloyd beat them with a made-up team that hadn't previously worked together. Steve continued that his dad had a way of communicating with dogs, which probably helped. They knew what he wanted, and they responded!

Rex was a prime example. As this book is being written, Lloyd's wife Alta is currently living with Steve in Oregon, and a daughter, Sara Dexter, resides near them. After Lloyd's death, to escape the pumice dust in the Crater Lake area, Alta lived in Alaska for a time for her health and mainly her lungs. Another daughter, Sandy, who won the Children's Race when she was 4 years old with Rex, who was almost 2 years old, died in an automobile accident in Hawaii in her mid-fifties.

ALTA AND STEVE VAN SICKLE,
JUST DAYS BEFORE THE REX BOOK GOES TO PRESS!
PHOTOGRAPH BY SARA VAN SICKLE DEXTER.
COURTESY SARA VAN SICKLE DEXTER.

On the Move

According to Steve, and along with the reminiscences of Alice Lombardi, Assistant Dog Show Photographer in the early 1950s, and Mel Fishback, Lloyd always talked while he moved away from you, and was always on the go.

In her Letter of Appreciation to Lloyd from the aforementioned *NDN,* Mel wrote:

[Lee and I] have known hundreds of drivers who deserve essays—good drivers and bad drivers and drivers who were simply personalities in their own right—interesting people. The person who (has) had the most effect on (my) career and that of (my) husband in the sled dog business was most certainly, Lloyd Van Sickle.... He affected not only (our) way with dogs, but indirectly, (the) dogs themselves. His opinions and attitudes stuck with them.

One of the nicest descriptions of Lloyd was a very long article from *Northern Dog News (NDN)* written in December 1974 by Mel Fishback, which is excerpted here. As you read through, I hope you appreciate the description. (Mel and Lee first heard of Lloyd, whom almost everyone called "Van," but not Mel because she talked so much to Alta and he was always "Lloyd" to her.)

"The first we heard about Lloyd was from the couple who sold [us our] first dog. Lloyd Van Sickle was the champion of all Samoyed drivers. He was the master, the pro; he was too big to compete with. He lived in a far off corner of California, but also seemed to be associated with the wild country of Montana and Idaho where he and his dogs performed their exploits in the racing world.

"We met him for the first time at a small race in Southern California, where he had brought the fabled Samoyed leader, Rex of White Way, to run with two borrowed dogs. He didn't even win the race. He seemed a sort of distant Informed Person who was here and there in the group, accompanied by a few who seemed to have special interest in his being there."

(Years later at the same event, Mel and Lee were at a Truckee gas station when they met up with Lloyd again. Lloyd invited them to move into one of his vacant cabins up at the Hilltop Lodge.)

"Lloyd is not the tallest person going but one of the most energetic! A half-hour in a chair without moving, without a trip to the door to clear the lip of a little used snuff appears to be agonizing. We always got the impression that inactivity really hurt. He was here and there, working on this and that, arguing with one person in town and dreaming up vast schemes with someone else."

(The Fishbacks lived across from the Van Sickles for the next four months and learned about dog driving.)

"We never found life in Truckee dull. Any quiet morning, while we were eating breakfast and sitting on the porch enjoying the winter sun over our twelve feet of snow, Lloyd might turn up to taunt Lee about dog driving. *Where's your team?* Our team would obviously be conked out on the stakeout line in front of the cabin. A mad rush would ensue, with Lee snapping in dogs at a great rate, only to find that Lloyd wasn't hooked up at all. In fact, he had decided not to run at all because the snow was too fresh and deep, the trails were all wiped out, and he wasn't in the mood anyway. But with all the dogs in harness, Lee would go anyway. And often Lloyd would hook up in lightening style because he couldn't stand the thought that Lee was really going to go, regardless of the conditions!

"Lee tried to drive his road-trained dogs in open snowfields with no success. Lloyd went out and showed him how to start a trail for them, how to come back without setting other trails, how to go to a dog that wasn't making an effort, what to do when he got to the dog. He taught the conditions a leader could be turned loose for the benefit of the whole team, when the dogs had to be hitched single file to make any progress at all, how to tell when a dog had had enough and when it was just being lazy or stubborn."

"He taught the idea of inciting wildness in the dogs, letting them think they were getting away with mayhem and craziness while they were only doing the right thing. He taught the driver to keep quiet when things were good, and how to make the right impression on the dogs when things were bad.

"He taught Lee how to make our dogs go anywhere—and do it willingly and gladly. He hooked visiting dogs that knew nothing, and got them working or at least moving when they had no inclination. He drove inexperienced dogs on trails many full-time racing dogs would refuse to tackle. He drove dogs by moonlight, in white-out blizzards, in snow so deep they sank so far they couldn't see ahead until they sprang up again. If he didn't feel like driving himself, he always conned someone else into driving.

"Lee swam dogs across the river, fell through snow-bridges, broke trail for twenty miles, just because Lloyd remarked he had done it, or it could be done, or it would be an interesting thing to do.

"His pride in the Samoyed Rex meant much more than most people would think, because he classed this particular dog with the best dogs he had driven.

"When he downgraded the dogs he was driving at that time, we could guess how good were the dogs he called good. His marvelous black leader, Jet, a Hound and Labrador cross, he classed as a good old dog, but with no stamina—yet we watched old Jet, doing it all, race after race and never refusing to try anything he was asked. We can only guess about the ability of Rex or Red—dogs we never saw at all or only saw as finished up old timers.

"Lloyd's love for back country driving, trail breaking, and impossible hauls paid off; although he never did the kind of concentrated training that every race driver endures or enjoys nowadays, he was hard to beat anywhere. He was the master of the art of convincing a lead dog he'd taken a turn all by himself, although the entire turn was accomplished by carrying the sled over, pulling back on the towline at strategic moments, praising at just the right moment and always keeping his attention.

"[Nobody] has taught us more about sled dogs, and perhaps the only reason we have had moderate success in the business is the winter we spent in Truckee shoveling snow off roofs, putting chains on cars, eating spaghetti and rice—and listening to Lloyd Van Sickle [talk about] dogs.

"Our greatest regret is that most of these people have put nothing permanent on paper or tape, for the sake of other sled dog fanciers; and we regret it most for Lloyd, because his memoirs would be the most entertaining as well as full of truth...."

"Here's to you, Lloyd—don't laugh too hard at the way we saw you."

LLOYD'S STORIES, AND HIS LIFE WITH REX, ARE NOW HERE—ENTERTAINING, INFORMATIVE, AND POIGNANT. THANK YOU, LLOYD, AND STEVE.

In her Letter of Appreciation addressed to the members of the Samoyed Club of America dated August 2, 1952, Agnes Mason also gives warm credit to Lloyd Van Sickle:

> Lloyd has done more than anyone to prove the Sam's usefulness and ability under rugged conditions. He worked with us off and on since the beginning of organizing a team. He has used them on mail runs in Idaho; in races where they were only seconds behind the winning Siberians—and won over them in 1949; he has used them to search for lost skiers; has pulled out airplanes which have been forced down and in various other rescue missions as well as exhibitions.
>
> Without the training he had given them in the snow, in blizzards and other difficult conditions, we could never have proven that show dogs are equal to any other—they can weather the elements when some others cannot endure with great success. It has also been proven that sled dogs are not vicious, as our dogs are well behaved in the show ring. In fact, Rex our lead dog wags his tail constantly and, judging by his smile, enjoys every minute in the ring.

Lloyd was asked in 2004 who his favorite lead dog was. He responded that the dog you are with that day is your favorite lead dog! Lloyd lived in the present and had a remarkable life full of achievements. He worked very hard for his many successes. He said he never had a problem with Mrs. Mason about training. He said, "She always thought 100% of what I did. She knew her dogs and you can't argue with someone that knows she's got a cow-hocked sucker there...you know...and she's admitted, so what the (heck)...we had nothing to argue about. They were her dogs and I was driving them ...and I broke 3 teams for her...maybe 4."

But the way he felt about Rex was special. He once said,

"As far as Rex's ownership was concerned, he was mine.
I owned him, but…she owned him, too…
you know what I mean…one of them deals.
I wouldn't take him from her
…but, actually, he was always my dog…."

LLOYD HOLDING "BABY REX" AT THREE MONTHS OLD, DECEMBER 1946.
COURTESY KAY KETCHUM.

YEARS LATER, LLOYD AND REX, THE MUSHER AND THE LEADER, IN DEEP SNOW IN IDAHO, HAVING THE TIME OF THEIR LIVES!

Lloyd passed away in December 2006.

**DEPICTIONS OF SAMOYEDS BRING JOY OF REMEMBRANCES,
AND GRACE THE HOMES OF MANY, INCLUDING JIM CHESKAWICH.
PHOTOGRAPH BY NOEL JOHNSON.
COURTESY JIM CHESKAWICH.**

TRUCKEE SLED DOG RACES, CIRCA 1925.
PRODUCED BY HAROLD McCOY.
ARTIST: KEN EBERTS.
USED BY PERMISSION OF HAROLD McCOY.

CHAPTER 4

THE ART AND TECHNIQUE OF TRAINING LEAD DOGS

To fully understand the difficulty and attributes to look for in training a lead dog, some background on sled dog training is essential to understanding the makeup of Rex.

Over the last half century or more, techniques have changed on training sled dogs, so what follows may be seen as more of a historical overview. Some of today's mushers do not use Lloyd's or Lee Fishback's training and working methods, as new techniques have been developed. Today sled dog camps are available for therapy, recreation, and adventure. Fifty-to-one-hundred-years-ago, sled dogs were used more for survival or to perform work that couldn't be accomplished by a machine. However, Lloyd and Lee were contemporaries, and what follows reflects how Rex was trained and how Lloyd and Lee viewed the lead dog in particular.

I rode horses for nearly eight years, often after sheepherding with my Samoyeds, enjoyed my jumping with my Clydesdale-Thoroughbred cross, and even evented once in Dressage with a Belgian Warmblood. I have been on the runners of a sled alone with 4 Samoyeds out in front of me at Burke Lake Park in Virginia. The feeling of power and control is unmatched.

I have also sat with a knowledgeable human partner on a diesel powered "vehicle" with 12 Samoyeds out front pulling us at a fairly good speed. With a horse, there is just you and one animal to worry about. With a sled dog team, there is potential for something to go wrong quickly—if you can even get them headed in the right direction! But you (the musher/dog driver) and the dogs are a team working together.

It is a rough life, but the lead dog and actually all members of the sled team are always treated special after the work is done. As Helen Corlew Newman of "Prairie Isle Dog Trekking" in North Dakota reminded me, you need a lead dog to "lead," but if you do not have willing team dogs, the team still will not go anywhere. She continued that "all the dogs, not just the lead dog, are special and have special jobs. It is tough being a sled dog no matter the position in the gangline! The team must trust the musher and want to please the human and when this occurs, then they all work together as a team." Helen thought there was too much emphasis placed in the old days on "outsmarting" a dog to get them to be a leader or be smarter than the leader. This approach comes through in Lloyd's interview and in Lee's book. Helen thought all members of the team need to be respected, to have them work together and the musher is part of the team, too!

Not every working dog can handle the physical and mental demands. Down through recorded history, there have been just a handful of lead dogs that have become internationally known. Etah, who possibly was a Samoyed, was believed for a long time to be the first to reach the South Pole on the Amundsen team. (However, there is information that has been recently uncovered that puts even that achievement in question.) Lead dogs for the winning team at the annual Iditarod Commemorative Race may get their picture in the papers with the winning musher and are quickly forgotten by the general public, but not by the sled racing community. Mushers will have multiple leaders so they can provide relief to the main leader. Each leader will have their own strength and weaknesses, too.

Lloyd's Words of Experience

Lloyd was asked in our interview, what makes a good lead dog? After the quick response, "He's gotta' be dumber than you are, then he gets to work." Then Lloyd got serious. "No, they're born, they're not broken. You don't break them, they're born to get out there. Well, it's rough you know. Most of them will go first, go down the road, around on the black top, with the wheels on the rig. Most of them will go right off on that, they want to go somewhere. Might be taking you in the park, but you get them to start and that's it. You have to show them what you want." Lloyd agreed that the secret to training is "to get the dog to do what you want the dog to do, but the dog has to think it's his idea."

He continued that "if you get one that ain't a born leader, you ain't got nothing. But another one that you got, put him on wheel, get him broke, and stick him out there some time in the front and you get yourself a surprise, take right off doing it as good as a lead, regular dog. You gotta' outsmart him, that's all."

OTHERS WEIGH IN

The following are a few insights by professionals in the field which I found to be both interesting and informative:

From *Mush, A Beginner's Manual of Sled Dog Training:*

Strength is not as important in sled dog racing as speed, since the sled load is distributed among many dogs. Large, heavily built dogs with great strength are not as fast as lean, wiry dogs; and they tend to tire sooner when asked to go fast. For comparison, human weight lifters don't run in marathon races." (We can see right away that Rex was different, as he had world class strength and was fast, very fast!)

For pure speed, the coursing hounds, fastest dogs on earth, would seem to be most desirable for pulling a sled. But speed without the stamina to maintain it does not count for much, so the Greyhounds, the Salukis, the Afghans and the Borzoi are not found in purebred form on the race trails. On the other hand, the moderately fast, long distance hounds developed for tracking coons for days on end have won many races, particularly in moderate to warm weather conditions. Many crosses of Husky and Greyhound have been attempted, particularly in eastern Canada.

From page 256 of the Bob and Dolly Ward book, *The New Complete Samoyed*:

> Possibly the greatest and best known of all sled dog drivers in the history of sledding was Leonhard Seppala, who died in 1967. Seppala was in partnership with Mrs. Margaret Ricker with a kennel of Samoyeds and Siberians in New Hampshire in the 1920s. Mrs. Ricker married the son of Fridtjof Nansen, the man who really brought the Samoyed dog to the notice of the [polar] explorers in the 1890s.
>
> Seppala organized the Race to Nome with the badly needed serum for a raging diphtheria epidemic, and a statue of his lead dog Balto, built with pennies collected by school children in America, stands in Central Park in New York City.... The serum run was made with a series of six teams and drivers which Seppala helped set up, and many of his stable of 122 dogs were the ones used in the various teams. Used as the lead dog on the last relay with the serum, Balto thereby received the total credit.

Several books on the "Serum Run" (even one that I read with the students in a recent 4th grade class at Yacolt Elementary School in Yacolt, Washington) indicate that Togo, the regular lead dog, made over 50% of the journey, but was not the lead dog at the end. Togo ended up crippled permanently as a result of his heroic contributions to the Serum Run and was largely forgotten for many years... but not here!

There are many valuable publications in print on how a lead dog is trained. Some are identified at the end of this book. Mushing magazines regularly feature articles on how to train a lead dog, deal with problems, as well as offering the latest advice on equipment, etc. One of the best publications still available was written by Lee and Mel Fishback and is entitled *Training Lead Dogs*.

UNDERSTANDING REX'S ROLE AS A LEAD DOG

It is important to the Rex story to understand a little of how a lead dog is trained, and why some make it and most do not. Among the highlights in their book, Lee Fishback mentions that it is no fun to finish every race with a seven-way fan hitch (seven dogs, with no Leader), or to own a whole kennel of fast dogs whose speed is only known because they've run full speed in the wrong direction so many times! The dog has to suit the driver's style. A highly trained leader often knows too much; the beginner driver can't keep up with him mentally. A key component to the Rex story is that Rex met up with Lloyd at just the right time. He was not ruined by someone else and he responded well to Lloyd's training techniques.

A 9-HITCH DOG TEAM. PORCELAIN PLATE, "CHRISTMAS IN GREENLAND"
(ROYAL COPENHAGEN, DENMARK).
PHOTOGRAPH BY NOEL JOHNSON. COURTESY JIM CHESKAWICH.

Lee states that the few people who can train leaders for other people must go to considerable pains to avoid becoming too close to the dog, and must train by a very carefully planned scientific method, unless they are blessed with unusually good material in the way of dogs with natural leadership and responsibility. Even the "naturals" are usually best for their original trainers whether their training is completely impersonal or not.

Here, Rex was the notable exception,as he also worked for Aljean Mason in the Conformation Ring! He also worked on occasion for Alta Van Sickle. However, with then-teenager and future California Governor Jerry Brown, back in the 1950s, Rex did not distinguish himself—see Chapter 10! There are many fabled leaders who wouldn't perform for a new driver the first year. Lee sums it up by saying that "…all you need is desire and stamina…which is all your dog needs too."

Helen Corlew Newman agrees up to a point that many leaders will not work for others than the one that trains them. "Once that lead dog trusts (as in a situation when a dog is sold to a different person) their new human, they usually will lead for them, but the trust must go both ways. There are sled teams out in the public all the time providing dog sledding experiences, and the dogs are trained to listen to other people. The leader knows its job once trained. It is the human that must learn to be part of the team." Natural born leaders do not come along on a regular basis. You can teach a dog that is willing to be in front to follow the musher's commands. But a natural leader knows their job with only a need for guidance from the musher on the command words.

Dog Sled. Courtesy Helen Corlew Newman.

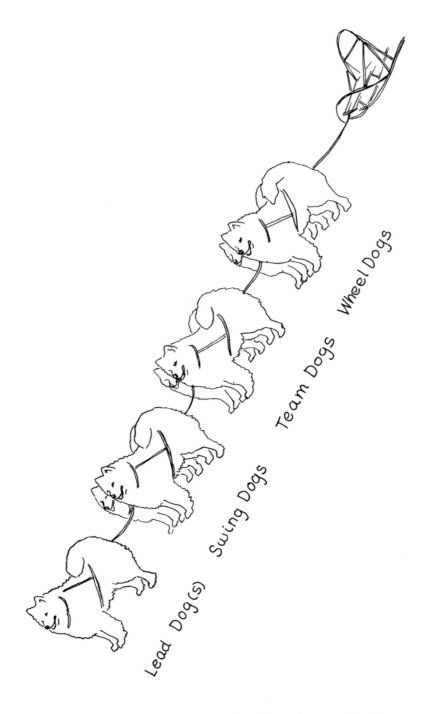

Wheel Dogs

Team Dogs

Swing Dogs

Lead Dog(s)

DOG SLED LINE-UP. ILLUSTRATION BY NAN HOLT. COURTESY NAN HOLT.

Helen L. Corlew   http://prairieisledogtrekking.com
12301 Hwy 2   prairieisle@gmail.com
Petersburg, ND 58272   701-345-8554

DOG SLEDDING TERMS

leaders: the first set of dogs in the team—they lead the team and listen for commands from the musher

swing dogs: dogs right behind the leaders. They help the leaders swing the team on turns

team dogs: dogs after the swing dogs and they help in turning and pulling.

wheel dogs: the dogs right in front of the sled. These dogs are the powerhouse dogs and very agile. They have to swing the sled around any corner plus move themselves out of the way. With the help of the team dogs they start the sled in motion from a stop.

runners: part of sled that moves across the snow

gangline: rope and/or cable device to hook sets of dogs together to the sled

brake: device to stop the sled

tugline: section of gangline for each dog that is hooked to the back of their harness

snowhook: metal, sharp object used to hold the team and sled in the winter time

neckline: short section of the gangline that attaches the collar/neck of the dog to the gangline

drag: piece of snowmobile track with very sharp points screwed into it and used to slow the team down when on snow

harness: what the dog wears so they can pull the sled. It fits snugly around their neck and across their shoulders and usually crosses over their back.

basket/bed: part of the sled that one can carry freight

booties: equipment used with the dogs to protect their feet from cuts and abrasions when running on ice, crystallized snow or gravel roads.

brushbow: front of the sled—similar to a bumper on a car. Helps absorb the shock if the sled hits something.

collars: sled dogs usually wear either limited slip or full circle collars that are made from heavy duty webbing.

stanchion: upright supports on a sled

footpads: nonslip pads placed on the top of the sled runners for the musher to stand on.

handle bar: usually the two rear stanchions continue to meet at a height that is comfortable for the musher to hold onto the sled. Place for the musher to hang onto the sled

sled bag: bag that fits the bed or basket of the sled so one can carry freight or a dog and things are protected from the weather.

bridle: cable or rope set up that connects the sled to the gangline.

whoa: used to tell the team to stop

gee: turn right

gee over: team is to move over to the right side of the trail

gee about: turn to the right and go back the same direction you came from. 180 degree turn to the right

haw: turn left

haw over: team is to move over to the left side of the trail

haw about: turn to the left and do a 180 degree turn.

easy: slow down and be careful

on-by: command used to tell the team to keep going forward and no stopping to sniff or visit.

line out and tighten up: command to have the dogs all pull forward so the gangline and their tugs are tight

hike/hup/let's go: different commands used to tell the team to go

From the Fishback book, the following represents what you are training for…and what a good leader *Should* do:

1. When your lead dog is hooked in front of a well-behaved team, or a small team, he keeps the towline taut between him and the sled, and stays in approximately the same spot he was placed by the driver. He takes up slack automatically, or whenever told to tighten up by the driver.

2. He watches for signs of imminent start, is in motion a fraction of a second before the rest of the team, and leaves the start in a perfectly straight line, with the towline taut behind him, looking neither right nor left.

3. He sets the pace for the entire team (in cooperation with the driver) and neither slacks off, letting the towline drop behind him, nor works unduly hard forcing the pace and exhausting himself. He keeps his tug just taut at all times. (In the long run, the lead dog will work—both physically and mentally—twice as hard as every other dog in the team. It is to the trainer's advantage NEVER to emphasize hard pulling in the leader.)

4. After the initial rush to keep the team strung out in their early enthusiasm, he will set a steady pace (usually a lope or slow gallop) and make every effort to maintain that particular gait, since his rhythm is copied by every other dog behind him.

5. On command, and only on command, he will swing the team Gee (right) and Haw (left) anyplace the driver indicates. He will do this without dropping back or stopping, or breaking gait as long as the trail is well defined and firm. (As Mel Fishback writes later in our story, Rex may have been the ultimate "Gee-Haw" dog.)

6. He will pass other animals and teams without hesitating or investigating, whether he approaches from the front or the rear (head-on or side-by-side).

7. He will urinate or defecate while in motion, without slowing down appreciably, and will not attempt to veer toward objects along the trail for these purposes.

8. He will stop on the command of "Whoa" without undue braking effort by the driver and will stand reasonably steady during trail stops, in the location where he was stopped, keeping the towline taut through any emergency.

9. He will obey "Straight ahead" or "On by" in a confusing intersection, or when driven in open untracked terrain.

10. He will continue to travel at the best possible speed until he is told "Whoa," never stopping voluntarily for any reason.

Lee Fishback continued on what good team leaders do *Not* do:

1. A good team leader will never drop back to "punish" lazy dogs in the team; in fact, he will never contact the rest of the team in any way.

2. He will not "use his own judgment" to select the best footing or decide whether to cross unsafe looking ground when there is a clear trail ahead of him. He will go where the driver directs him to go at all times. A human being is more intelligent about where a team, sled, and driver may safely travel than any dog!

   (Although Lee says this in his book, and it is presumably how Rex was trained by Lloyd, Helen Corlew Newman disagrees and feels many of today's mushers also would disagree. "The driver trusts the lead dog and if that lead dog refuses or changes course, then it is time for the driver to think (so stop the team if needed), and figure out why the change. Mutual respect and trust—being mindful—has to be present between the leader and the musher. Mushers have a very deep bond with their dogs; it goes both ways. That's why mushers are able to ask the dogs to perform some of the things they do and the dogs willingly do—trust and respect.")

3. He will not be "team boss" and will not fight with members of his own team or any other team if he can avoid it in any way.

4. He will not return to his fallen driver when the driver loses the sled. His entire training is devoted to keeping the team strung out and moving fast, except when the driver gives distinct commands directing him to bring them around in a reverse direction. Many good leaders are never taught a command to reverse. (We will see later a perfect example of how Rex took the team on a 16-mile "jaunt" without Lloyd, who had been knocked unconscious and was left behind on the mail run! Rex brought the team back, and woke Lloyd up with his face-licking.)

5. He will never be as reliable or perfect as Lassie or Rin-Tin-Tin if he lives to be 20. This is a demanding job and he will sometimes want "out" of it. And unlike Lassie, he will be on-camera and watched every minute he is in harness. Lead Dog Maintenance never stops!

Lee continues: "The lead prospect may be outgoing, timid, friendly, or reserved...but should love to run and must respond to training commands. It is much easier if the prospect is relaxed around other dogs or is generally uninterested in them. The trainer must be in as good condition as the dog.

"Natural leaders are grand to work with. It will never occur to this dog to fall in behind another team, slack off to join his teammates, or drop back next to the driver. The natural leader has no desire to make himself uncomfortable by working harder than conditions easily allow. Unless his natural abilities are placed under restraint by the driver, he will take complete charge of where the team goes, how fast it goes, and the distance it will continue to travel. That driving such a dog is a very chancy business has been proven many times by people who one day, one year found themselves stranded, many miles from home with a total quit in progress—because 'Mr. Natural' decided that it was hole-digging time, not blizzard-facing time."

HAVING THE RIGHT ATTITUDE

As Lee states: "Attitude in a sled dog can best be described as an expression of eagerness and positiveness demonstrated by a dog that knows he is going to do a tiring job. An eighteen-month-old dog with six races under his belt, all of them a little tougher and longer than befitted his age, that still bounces and sing-songs at every hookup or trail stop has attitude. Knowing that a dog can maintain his good spirits and enjoyment of the game even when he's been pressed to the limit is a real asset when choosing a lead prospect. Attitude is an acquired trait that can be seen only in dogs that have experienced the bad days as well as the good ones."

Rex showed attitude and aptitude from an early age. Lloyd gave him a lot of good positive experiences early on so that Rex was very quickly acting and assuming the role of a well-trained veteran lead dog even though he was only 2 or 3 years of age.

HARNESSING...AND UNHARNESSING

As Bob and Dolly Ward explain in their book, harnessing and unharnessing are times when great problems occur unless you have a consistent system which the dogs understand. A good method they suggest is to fasten the main gangline to the sled and stretch it out upon the ground. "Anchor your gee line to a post or stake in the ground. The gee line runs from the tug line ring to the driver, usually under the sled, and trails loosely. With the sled thus secured, a runaway team is prevented. Now the leader is hitched with the command Stay or Hold It. This keeps the tug line taut and prevents the remaining dogs from becoming tangled. With all dogs harnessed, place the steadier dogs in the team first and command, Down to each as they are hitched in place. Do not hitch up a team too long before you intend to start, as the dogs' natural eagerness to go will be lost."

Helen Corlew Newman said to me that the leader is hooked up first and then normally you hook in your swing dogs (behind the leaders who are back-up leaders), and work your way back to the wheel dogs. Each musher has his own system to hooking their team into the gangline. An example is adding the calmest dogs first and then the more energetic ones last. Teaching the team, not just the leader(s), to line out, wait, stay, and to be patient makes hook-up an easier task.

In unharnessing a team, as the Wards explain, "The sled must be anchored from the rear by fastening the gee line to a post or tree. It is interesting to note that Leonhard Seppala carried a metal rod which he drove through a hole in his brake lever, deep into the snow to hold his team on every halt. Many drivers merely turn the sled on its side. Unharnessing usually begins with the swing and point dogs, as the wheel dogs cannot be very easily entangled with others as they are fastened to the sled, and thus cannot go very far sideways or backwards."

WHEEL DOGS

Having strong, smart wheel dogs is just as important as a good leader! It is those wheel dogs that actually help the musher/driver turn the sled properly. If the lead dog does cut corners, the wheel dogs and teams dogs, in front of the wheelers, are the dogs that make it possible to steer the sled properly and safely.

ONWARD WITH REX

So now, with this as essential background, we can continue with our story!

A key component to the Rex story is that Rex met up with Lloyd at just the right time. He was not ruined by someone else and he responded well to Lloyd's training techniques. Lee states that the few people who can train leaders for other people must go to considerable pains to avoid becoming too close to the dog, and must train by a very carefully planned scientific method, unless they are blessed with unusually good material in the way of dogs with natural leadership and responsibility. Even the "naturals" are usually best for their original trainers whether their training is completely impersonal or not.

Lloyd Van Sickle said at least once in the interview that our production team conducted with him in 2004 "...great sled dog team leaders are born and not made. Some have it and some don't, it takes you a long time to get'em 'til they got it, and the other one that's got it, you don't have to work with him, he's already there. I can remember the first time I hooked him (Rex), I just...you got a picture of him and that's it." Lloyd said elsewhere in the interview, "He's gotta' know what you want before you can make him do it."

Lloyd knew how to bring out Rex's natural leadership qualities. Rex's uncommon strength and speed coupled with his leadership made him a force of nature when positioned in front of a team.

"With my mouth and his muscle, we go where we want to go," *Lloyd said.*

Like the baseball movie with Robert Redford in the 1980s, Rex was "The Natural"...and all the dogs knew it.

Lloyd said that Rex beat them all when he had to find a trail. "When it got too deep, he'd go down and walk on the bottom...he didn't care. You couldn't tell whether he was on it (the trail) or off...you know...but he'd get his snoot down there low and come out there and look at you and...and his head was all full of snow...and his eyes and ears...he just puts his head down and lets the snow blow over him."

As testament to his adaptability, because Chattigan couldn't make the jump, Rex was "drafted" in his place and he won the Kid's Race at age two with the Van Sickle's four-year-old daughter, Sandy! This picture of Sandy and Rex in Ashton, Idaho in 1948 was picked up by the media, and was syndicated and appeared in 75 newspapers nationally! Fan mail started coming in from as far away as Louisiana, among other places. Courtesy Sara Van Sickle Dexter.

CHAPTER 5

THE EARLY REX YEARS: 1946–1951

Since it has been some 55 years since Rex was on the scene, I started thinking about "the world" as it was during his time here with us. *As A Backdrop* I present these few "glimpses" into the past, which "old-timers" like me remember and "newcomers" since them might enjoy.

As A Backdrop...

During 1946, Winston Churchill employed the term "Iron Curtain" in a speech. The Philippines were given independence by the U.S. on July 4. One hundred years before, in 1846, the Donner Party of 87 American pioneers set out by wagon train for California—an event which was to gain new importance a few years later. Frank Sinatra, Bing Crosby, Perry Como, and the Andrews Sisters were popular musicians.

In 1947, Jackie Robinson joined the Brooklyn Dodgers on April 11, breaking the color barrier in major league baseball. Air Force Captain Chuck Yeager broke the sound barrier in the X-1 rocket plane. The transistor was invented, and Polaroid's Land Camera developed photos in 60-seconds.

In 1948, President Harry Truman was elected on November 2, defeating Governor Thomas Dewey in historic upset. *The Treasure of the Sierra Madre* with Humphrey Bogart and Walter Houston appears on screen, and *South Pacific* was on Broadway. Gas was 16-cents a gallon! (Source for all *Backdrops*: *The World Almanac* and *Book of Facts 2012,* and *American Decades,* 1940–1949; 1950–1959.)

Rex: 1946–1948

Rex was born on September 26, 1946. He was a first generation breeding of English imports through his imported father, sire Ch. White Way of Kobe and his dam, Ch. Herdsman's Faith, sired by imported Spark of the Arctic. The breeders were Mrs. Agnes Mason and Miss Aljean Mason. There were 4 males and 6 females in the litter. This was the third litter out of the breeding of Ch. White Way of Kobe and Ch. Herdsman's Faith. (White Way of Kobe sired at least 7 litters for the Mason's and records show that Faith produced 6 litters. Nowadays, those considered responsible breeders do not breed a single bitch more than 1–3 times, depending on all the right circumstances. Not every bitch should be bred; even among purebreds.)

Alta Van Sickle told me in 2004 that Rex was born a long legged, gangly pup, so Agnes Mason decided not to keep him to show him in the Conformation Ring.

Lloyd told us in the interview that "Mrs. Mason kept me pretty busy...breaking some in and then there was...this big pup (Rex) and he's oversize...he's long legged...and sloppy footed (Lloyd laughed) and he's everything you wouldn't want in a pup.

"Anyway, she sent him to me to hide him, I think...I, oh I shouldn't say that...I shouldn't tell you all the stuff I think...but...she had me take him to Truckee to ah, get him out of sight...and then started working on his height...he was too high...and she was President of the club, the Samoyed Club at that time...and about 50 meetings, why, they raised the standard up to Rex's size! Now...uh...I don't think I can prove it, but she surely could...I took him for her to get rid of him, I think, because he was oversized. But she stayed with me on him. At some point, after Rex had been away growing coat and growing up, she had him shown at dog shows, as he had become an impressive specimen, and the height standard had been raised so he could now be competitive in the Conformation Ring."

As Lloyd continued in the interview, "Rex was a good dog. Well, I'm kind'a prejudiced, too...I raised him. They were gonna' get rid of him because he was...(I shouldn't say that...maybe I shouldn't get that on record)...oversized. A little too big...but they got the standard up there. Now he is the standard. The standard's set on him, the last I knew. They just made him legal."

Mel Fishback said in her article in *NDN* that Lloyd showed her a few pictures of the "young Rex" and she could "see" why the young Rex was given to Lloyd by Mrs. Mason. "His hindquarters were long and angulated like a Shepherd; his forelegs came down together under the brisket, and, at a year old, his coat looked not much longer than a Siberian's."

She also wrote, in the *Organization for Working Samoyeds (OWS) The Yapper* in August 1972:

> Lloyd told [me] that Rex was a faulty pup; he had a very narrow front, and to quote Lloyd word-for-word: "His front legs came out of the same hole." He had the typical White Way male coat, very short and bushy in the places where he had any hair length. He had lots of angulation, but was still high in the rear. He was never light boned, but never gave the appearance of being a heavy boned dog, either.

Rex was over the height standard for that time. Later, the standard was raised, but Agnes couldn't possibly anticipate this at the time of "farming out" Rex to make him of "some use." At some point early on as a juvenile male, Rex was "loaned" to Lloyd Van Sickle in Idaho for training as a work dog. Because of all the descriptions that have come down to us of the "young Rex," and confirmed by Lloyd in the 2004 interview, Agnes probably thought that Rex was an embarrassment to her breeding program.

But Lloyd soon realized Rex's leadership abilities and was glad that he wasn't shown. It gave him more time to train him. Lloyd said that Rex handled the other dogs differently from other lead dogs he had. "He developed into a (heck) of a dog. He always ran with his head a little bit low...and his tail down...he didn't curl his tail up like most of them...high-heading them, you know. There was more power and he was calmer. When you got one going along barking off on everybody's yard then you ain't got nothing."

Rex developed into a beautiful Samoyed. He had an especially beautiful head, with more slanted eyes that Alta thought he had inherited from his sire, Ch. White Way of Kobe. He could run fast enough to lead the Hound team. That is very fast and...his long legs helped!

Lloyd said: "Other dogs would go out in deep snow and when they couldn't see over the top of that snow, some like old Lucky would turn around and come right back to the team, just a' snarling and a'snapping. Then I would put Rex out front. Rex would go down, smell the track...and walk on...get on it...and move the team."

That's where Rex was like the magic trump card...able to save the day or get them back to civilization.

REX, SAVING THE DAY!

Both Alta and her daughter, Sara, remember Rex as an endearing and constant companion. Sara said that they only had working dogs, and she didn't realize there was any other kind until she was a teenager! Sara remembered that Rex got to run loose and was always following the kids around. Most of the rest of the dogs were always tied up. Some of them lacked manners...taking off and killing the neighbor's chickens, or get into some other kind of trouble.

Rex was always keeping track of the kids. If they were on foot or horseback, Rex was there. Rex got used to roaming around and being carefree.

Rex completed Lloyd's training program tailored for him and was found to possess special qualities of intelligence, aptitude, attitude, and...leadership.

Lloyd had a job for him after all. He was "useful"...and needed!

EARLY RACES

As Lloyd said in his interview, natural leaders are born with it! As with all top lead dogs, Rex developed an early talent for judging the length of his team. Before making a turn, he would look back, and then gauge the width needed to swing the team around a tree or corner. (Otherwise, the entire team gets surprised with a sudden jerk and halt caused by wrapping the sled around a tree!)

"REX TO THE RESCUE!!!"

The following is a summary of a radio broadcast in which Mrs. Mason took part in Sacramento, CA on March 14, 1948. The broadcast was sponsored by a local dog-food concern. The purpose of the broadcast was to give a firsthand picture of the tests which the U.S. Army was conducting to establish the feasibility of using sled dogs to haul sled and supplies and medicine for the rescue of stranded flyers who might otherwise perish.

From the May 1948 *Western Kennel World (WKW)* magazine:

The experiment was made on February 23rd at Ashton, Idaho, the day of the American Dog Derby Association's sled races. The teams, one of which was flown to Ashton, involved two Sacramento teams from Mrs. Mason's kennels. One team, sled dogs and driver, were carried aloft to 1,400 feet. On the ground were Mrs. Mason and the other team ready to go with Lloyd Van Sickle as the driver. Well, the plan was to parachute the driver and full team of five dogs to the appointed ground spot.

Lewis Price, of Felton, Idaho, driver of the first team—and with a record of 17 previously successful jumps for the Army—made the jump first. Then the sled was dropped—then one dog followed by two more. Watching the dogs on the way down was a breath-taking experience for the interested watchers.

The other two dogs were not allowed to go, for before the pilot could maneuver the plane back in position at the 1,400 foot level, the wind had increased so much that he considered it an unnecessary risk to which to subject the dogs. So, two of the seven dogs from Van Sickle's team were switched to the other team and they were ready for the race.

When the plane flew off with the dogs, it (seemingly) carried with it little four-year-old Sandra Van Sickle's hope of entering the Children's One-Dog Team Race. Chattigan, Sandra's proposed White Way Samoyed dog, was still in the plane.

In making the parachute leaps, the dogs didn't seem to be a bit afraid—in fact, the one that came down following the sled saw a rabbit just as he landed and had to be restrained to prevent him from chasing it. Another was seen to wag his tail as he came down.

In order to be prepared for the grueling race—and to accustom them to the ice and snow—the Mason team had been trained for the odds. Lloyd Van Sickle has had some of the dogs since last spring, when he was using them when he took over the job of carrying mail out of Drummosa, Idaho, a rural mail route.

REX'S ATTRIBUTES

Alta said that Rex was adaptable. She and Lloyd both said that he was always serious and responsible. Alta remembered him in her mind...waiting to start, straining to hold the tow line taut, while his teammates jumped and barked excitedly behind him.

As Lloyd has stated, Rex always led with his head down, to follow the trail, and his tail was usually down, too, when working. Others kept their heads high while working lead, which made them more easily distracted by crowds and made it tougher for them to see in the falling snow. Alta thought Rex's slanted eyes helped him go through blizzards.

Both Alta and Sara remembered Rex as a special dog.

SANTA CLAUS

During Christmas, Lloyd Van Sickle used the Samoyeds to haul Santa Claus to visit the children of Ashton. A large photograph of Mrs. Van Sickle with Rex of White Way was a favorite with the Utah Press. In one article it was noted that "Rex has the true Mongel-slant eyes that stamp the breed, and a lovely head with not too thin ears."

THE CALIFORNIA STATE FAIR

The following appeared in the November 1948 *WKW* magazine extolling Agnes Mason's team led by Rex at the California State Fair: "Sled racing is the oldest sport in the world, almost, and yet for our breed (Samoyeds), one of the newest. To date, Mrs. Mason, and a few California owners who have sent their dogs to Idaho, are the only owners engaging in the sport. It is a field for sportsmen and sportswomen, with new fields to conquer, new honors to win, new thrills to experience. It's a sport once in, you are sunk—it gets you and you are in for keeps."

The California State Fair is one of the largest in the nation. As the *WKW* reported, the young team with Rex at lead did very well. Rex had previously been used only in snow and blizzards. Behind the scenes, Lloyd, thinking that Chat (Ch. Herdsman's Chattigan) would be even better as a leader, changed the leaders...which caused a little (dog) hair pulling. Topper, it seems, resented a new leader...he wanted Rex as his leader!

The *WKW* magazine article gives it a "wrap!"

After the exhibition of the team racing, the dogs were unleashed from the sled and children were allowed to take the dogs around the fair grounds on leashes, which brought further admiration from the crowds and much petting for the dogs.... The group was also televised... "giving us a chance to broadcast and answer questions on the breed," said Mrs. Mason.

It is apparent from this little vignette that Topper preferred Rex early on as his leader. At the time of Mrs. Mason's comments/write-up on Rex and Chattigan at the State Fair, Chattigan was the steady and proven veteran leader, but there were already indications of greatness for young Rex based on his performance in blizzards and the mail run. Topper knew it, sensed it and wanted his choice for leader out front at the State Fair!

Lloyd told us in his interview that no one challenged Rex as leader and no one growled at him. He was respected as pack leader and was calm throughout his work.

REX: 1949–1951

As A Backdrop...

Rex is 3 years old in 1949 when the North Atlantic Treaty Organization (NATO) was established August 24. President Truman on October 26 signed legislation raising the federal minimum wage from 45-cents-an-hour to 75-cents an hour. Arthur Miller's *Death of a Salesman* opened on Broadway. The first commercially available computer was released. George Orwell's *1984* is published. Hank Williams debuts at "Grand Ole Opry."

In 1950, President Truman authorized production of the H-bomb. North Korean forces invaded South Korea June 25, and President Truman ordered U.S. Air Force and Navy to Korea on June 27. Charles Schulz's *Peanuts* comic strip first appears in newspapers on October 2, and the Diners Club issues the first credit card.

In 1951, the 22nd Amendment, limiting a U.S. President's term of office, was ratified February 27. The Korean fighting ends officially on July 27, 1953, with the peace treaty signed in San Francisco September 8. J. D. Salinger's *Catcher in the Rye* is published. The first color television show is broadcast from the Empire State Building. "Rock 'N Roll" as a phrase is coined by Alan Freed, and *The African Queen* with Humphrey Bogart and Katherine Hepburn, and *An American in Paris* with Gene Kelly and Leslie Caron, are on the screen.

Down the road from Agnes Mason and Rex at the University of San Francisco—after an undefeated football season and high national ranking—the team voted not to go to any of the three southern Bowl Games because their two black stars, Ollie Matson and Burl Tolar, weren't invited. The team produced a still-unmatched 10 starters in the NFL, and contributed three future Hall of Famers: Ollie Matson, Gino Marchetti, and Bob St. Clair. Significantly, football was dropped in 1952, as the University made a statement for integration.

1949 was a busy year for Rex, characterized by wins at local sled races, participation in parades and exhibitions, and leading "rescue missions," including that of passengers involved in an horrific plane crash at the Truckee Airport.

First up, in March, were two "friendly matches" in Truckee and in Tahoe City, with "The Donner Trail Association" sponsoring a team of racing dogs to challenge the drivers of the "Mason-Van Sickle team."

The February 1949 issue of the *WKW* reported:

Mrs. Mason's 11 Sams are at the kennels at Hilltop Lodge, together with a team of Irish Setters owned by Van Sickle. Wm. Rutherford is president of the Association, and over in Tahoe City, Constable Harry Johnson has a team of Huskies well trained in rescue and racing work." It went on to quote portions from the *Sacramento Bee:* "The presence of the racing dogs has lent a colorful innovation to the scene at Truckee with Van Sickle and his dogs a daily sight on the mountain community street since snow first fell."

The U.S. Forest service has appointed a promotional director to oversee and aid in all winter sports throughout Tahoe National Forest. The Southern Pacific Railroad [has] got up posters to advertise the March 5–6 races and is offering special rates to passengers attending the races. They have been publicized as never before.

The April-May *Bulletin of the Samoyed Club of America* followed up with a feature story on the *success* of the Mason-Van Sickle team with the headline: "Champion Retains Dog Sled Racing Title at Truckee." Quoting the *Sacramento Bee* (this time of March 7), it reported:

Lloyd Van Sickle of Truckee remains the national 11-mile dog sled racing champion after posting a combined two-day time for the event of fifty-eight minutes and fifty-seven and one-half seconds. Lloyd successfully defended his crown Saturday and yesterday in the Sierra Dog Derby, beating out his brother Bob, of Cascade, Idaho, driving a team of Malamutes. Bob had a combined time of fifty-nine minutes and eleven-seconds. Lloyd's team had nine purebred Samoyeds owned by Mrs. A .E. Mason of Winding Way, Sacramento, California—the lead dog being Rex of White Way. More than five hundred spectators were on hand Saturday for the opening and approximately one thousand for Sunday's wind up.

…The most spectacular moment in the two-day derby came Sunday as Bob Van Sickle fought out the second spot with third place winner Lewis Price of Teuton Basin, Idaho, who drove a team of the Mason Sams, with Nick of White Way as Leader.

1949 TRUCKEE PLANE RESCUE AND OTHER RESCUES

Rex was the Leader of the rescue team to a plane crash at Truckee, California pulling out men from one downed planes. He was also the Leader when pulling out the downed plane. The Spring *SCA Bulletin* addressed the plane rescue at Truckee and also referred to the February 1949 issue of *Popular Mechanics,* where Lloyd and the sled team were written up for their wins in racing and also the rescue of the downed Truckee plane. It was reported that Lowell Thomas "murdered" the word "Samoyed" in his newscast on the plane rescue.

Lloyd said he loaded the most injured man on the sled. "It was a guy who had two mouths...his teeth came right through there! See...what happened is when they come over from Frisco, they go to Reno...all of them liquored up good and oiled up. When they come over and (try) to clear the top of the mountain...(they sail) into that fog up there, and they ice up...and then they're heading for Reno. (But) you can't make that, so you dive into that (Truckee) airport there. It's got some crusted snow in there. When the wheels hit and they lock up...well, they tip over. Dr. Nelson worked on the guy a little with teeth coming through his mouth."

THE SA

Maoris -

Founded 1857   C   SACRAMENT

Dog Teams Rescue Four Men After Crash Landing On Snowfield At Truckee

(McClatchy Newspapers Service)

TRUCKEE (Nevada Co.), Feb. 1. — Three passengers and a pilot whose chartered plane crash landed in the snow, continued on to Reno by automobile today following their rescue by dog teams and sleds. The passengers, all San Franciscans, escaped serious injury. They are Morris Murphy, 52; his son, James, 23, and William O'Neill, 50. The pilot, Floyd Sanchez, 35, of San Lorenzo, was unhurt.

MUSH!—AFTER CHESTER WRIGHT OF UKIAH, MENDOCINO COUNTY, WRECKED HIS SMALL AIRPLANE IN A FORCED LANDING ON THE TRUCKEE EMERGENCY AIRPORT—IN WHICH HE ESCAPED INJURY—HE CALLED UPON LLOYD VAN SICKLE AND LEWIS PRICE, DOG TEAM DRIVERS, TO PULL THE PLANE TO THE HIGHWAY WHERE IT COULD BE REMOVED FOR REPAIRS. ABOVE THEY ARE SHOWN WITH THEIR NINE SAMOYEDE DOG TEAM HAULING THE AIRPLANE OFF THE AIRPORT. THE TEAM IS THE ONE WHICH WON THE SIERRA DOG DERBY EARLY THIS MONTH. IT HAS HAULED TWO OTHER PLANES FROM THE FIELD DURING THE WINTER.

Plane Turns Over

Sanchez said the motor failed at 10,000 feet and the plane started down. He attempted to land on the snowbound Truckee Emergency Airfield but could not and the plane was set down on the hard crusted snow in a nearby clearing. It turned over.

The bruised and shaken passengers and the pilot wallowed through snow 3 feet deep for a half mile to an unoccupied cabin.

Tractor Fails

A witness saw the plane go down at 6:45 PM and notified Deputy Sheriff Fosten Wilson, who called out the Truckee patrol of the Nevada County Sheriff's Ski Posse. After a tractor bogged down the patrol enlisted the services of Lloyd Van Sickle and Edward Crandall, dog team drivers here in training for the Sierra Dog Derby, March 5th and 6th.

Dr. Lawrence Nelson went in on one sled and gave first aid: He found the quartet exhausted and the passengers suffering from shock. Several stitches were required to close a cut on Morris Murphy's face. The four were taken out on sleds, arriving here at 10 o'clock.

Near Air Tragedy Scene

Sanchez said he believes the carburetor iced, killing the motor. The group chartered the plane in Hayward and were on a pleasure trip to Reno.

The emergency landing field is four miles from Truckee and four miles west of where a C47 plane crashed in March, 1946, killing 26 persons, mostly soldiers returning home on discharge or furlough.

OTHER 1949 ACTIVITIES

Rex was the Leader in "Hauling Dudes" (a work crew). Rex was also the Leader when going into the Cedars Rescue. Rex was also the Leader going into the Ever Valley snow removal.

Another piece that covered the "early Rex" is from the July 1949 *WKW*, which noted that "the Mason Dog Team was exhibited at the Los Angeles Sportsman's Show for 10 days—and is booked for San Diego." (The *Western Kennel World Samoyed* column sometimes gave just a line or two on an activity; other times a full report was provided.)

As Bob and Dolly Ward pointed out in their book, *The New Complete Samoyed*, on page 255, a summation of the activities of Rex of White Way with his trainer and driver Lloyd Van Sickle further shows the versatility and endurance of a trained dog. Among the activities were: the three-exhibitions-a-day at the Sportsman's Show and the three-a-day, with the team pulling a calliope through the grounds at the San Diego Exposition. This calliope had been pulled earlier with four ponies...and the nine dogs handled it very well!

Agnes Mason and Lloyd ensured that the dogs continued with their training, health checkups, and that the sled and equipment were serviceable to perform the necessary work function. Entry fees and paperwork had to be submitted well in advance. It seems to me as if it was easier to exhibit the Samoyeds at parades over 50 years ago! To contrast, I tried to enter a team of four Samoyeds in the April Cherry Blossom Parade in the mid 1990s in Washington, DC and I was told that my request wasn't compatible with the intent and history of the Cherry Blossom Parade. Agnes Mason would probably have found a way to get her Samoyeds in the Cherry Blossom Parade.

1950 "HOMECOMING" AT UNIVERSITY OF CALIFORNIA, BERKELEY

We were able to find a detailed write-up of Rex's encounter with the "Berkeley Bear."

The following is from the January 1951, *WKW*, by Vera Lawrence, Editor:

An item from the *Daily Californian* published at the University of California in Berkeley on Friday, November 24, 1950 reads: "Red apples, blue and gold roses, and pure white sled dogs will be featured attractions in Eshleman Court today. The 'Devour the Red' apples and roses pertain to football, the dogs to this afternoon's Homecoming parade.

The team of seven purebred Siberian Samoyeds (not Huskies) will enter Eshleman Court at noon where they remain on display until time for their parade. At 3 p.m. they will take their places before a sled on wheels and trot down a parade route under the direction of driver Lloyd Van Sickle. The dogs have been brought to the campus by the U.C. Ski Club and have been used at A.S.U.C. Ski Lodge and Donner Summit resorts. The dogs are loyal Californians too, having covered themselves with blue ribbons (emphasis added) in many national and world contests. They also hold the 1949 Truckee Dog Derby championship. We understand that outside of Eshleman Hall the U.C. Ski Club had set up two easels on which appeared a concise history of the Sam as well as pictures, which attracted much attention.

The Sams received a rousing reception when they carried "Oski" (the California team mascot) and led the band to the Rally at the Greek Theatre. The dogs enjoyed the entire procedure, including the petting given them by admirers. However, when Oski got in their midst, Rex the lead dog, couldn't fathom such a character with the smell of a human, yet the head of a bear. The band, the firecrackers, etc., the dogs seemed to accept as part of the game—but Oski was something else again!]

The *Oakland Tribune* carried some pictures of the affair and thanks to the efforts of my sister, Ina Lawrence, we have some very enjoyable motion pictures in color of the team in the parade. With harness bedecked with the California colors—huge orange pompoms, they made quite a stunning sight.

"OSKI" THE BERKELEY BEAR, WITH FRIEND.
COURTESY THE BANCROFT LIBRARY, UNIVERSITY OF CALIFORNIA, BERKELEY.
USED BY PERMISSION.

1951 "SHOWTIME" AND...
"REX, *THE GREAT ESCAPE ARTIST!*"

Agnes appears to have liked the grown-up Rex at some point because she cleaned him up and started putting him in dog shows with Aljean. As Lloyd told us in the interview, Rex had a short coat from working all the time in harness. It is very likely he also showed harness marks on his coat most of the time from his work life. Rex did pretty well at the shows but he just didn't get to enough shows to finish his championship. The following write-up reflects how he did in the show world:

From the December 1951 *WKW* magazine:

Rex has been the lead dog of the team for four years—has been shown only four times—Reserve once, Winners Dog twice, and once Best of Breed. Rex does not carry a long coat, but has the correct weather resisting type coat.

He is most friendly in the ring, wagging his tail all the time. One judge said Rex demonstrated the correct Samoyed disposition we want for our breed. Practically all of the judges who have seen him spoke of his excellent gait—the type for a work dog.

Sacramento was an unbenched show, meaning the dog didn't have to stay there the entire time until the end of the show. Since Rex took Best of Breed, he had to wait for the Working Group for his next appearance in the ring that day.

Before time for the Working Group judging, the Masons returned home with the other dogs, Rex and Starctic Jill among them. Proving that you can keep the dog out of the country just so long, Rex and Jill went on a run! When the Masons found them after an hour's search, face, legs and the under body hairs were so dirty—they didn't even resemble Sams.

Well, with time so short, Rex got the quickest surface cleaning he ever had. As Agnes reported, "We hosed the dirt and mud off him—rubbed him with towels—alcohol and dusted some boric acid powder into his coat—this we find helps to dry it—and arrived at the show during the judging of the Sporting Group. We allowed Rex to rest. As they usually chase squirrels, etc., sometimes even the pretty black and white cats, we were lucky he was not perfumed (sprayed by a skunk) —the thing we feared might happen!

"Rex showed beautifully—and no one would have guessed the ordeal all of us had been through shortly before."

There were considerably more bench shows 50–55 years ago, and Westminster, NY in February is practically the last AKC benched show remaining. At a benched show, your dog shows up early before the show starts and is expected to stay there all day until after the entire show is over. With today's on-the-move society, a lot of exhibitors are into show-and-go mode unless they move up to Group or Best in Show competition. Then they have to stay longer until eliminated. Rex was expected to stay all day at a benched show as it was not an option to leave early.

THE CEDARS RESCUE

As reported in an undated *Western Kennel World (WKW)* magazine, around this time Rex was involved in what became known as the "Cedars Rescue." According to Steve Van Sickle, Rex had to leave the Golden Gate dog show along with 2 of his kennel mates (one of the Samoyeds had just taken "Best of Breed") to be flown to Truckee to lead and break trail with a 9-dog team and Lloyd to rescue a couple (Roy and Jessie Thompson) who managed the ski resort.

(AUTHOR'S NOTE: One AKC judge told me that a dog would lose all its points, ribbons, and trophies it had earned that day—if the dog left a benched show without sound reason that had to be approved. Another AKC judge advised me that the local show-giving club may have its own policy which could expand on the above penalty—if a dog just was taken out of the benched show without Superintendent or Breed judge approval.)

Soda Springs is about 18-miles from Truckee, according to Steve, and things can come to a standstill in the higher elevations pretty quickly when it snows. The couple had been holed up for weeks, supplies were getting lower, and the call came in to Lloyd to get the couple out quickly, so Rex was called for the rescue! At the show, Rex was "Reserve Winner's Dog." The Thompsons were probably impressed with his flashy ribbon, but more grateful that Rex led them out of danger. This is a *working breed.*

As we can see, at just 3 years old, Rex had already begun to make his name in the world.

RUSSIAN CERAMIC.
PHOTOGRAPH BY NOEL JOHNSON.
COURTESY JIM CHESKAWICH.

Picking up air mail in Idaho for fast delivery by dog team. Driver, Lloyd Van Sickle, trainer for White Way Samoyeds. At lead, Rex of White Way.

PLEASE NOTICE REX'S **LONG LEGS...**
AN ASSET FOR CARRYING MAIL THROUGH THE DEEP SNOWDRIFTS!
COURTESY CAROL CHITTUM.

CHAPTER 6

THE MAIL
MUST GO THROUGH!

According to Steve Van Sickle, Rex was used on the mail run for a period of time as the lead dog. But Steve does not recall ever being on the run with his dad, Lloyd. The trip was often made at night and could take 3-1/2 to 4 hours. When Rex was at lead there was usually a team of 7 to 12 dogs on the run. Sometimes two teams were combined, as the run carried the U.S. mail, milk, and food for the people in West Yellowstone.

The run was so difficult that one time Lloyd fell about 9-feet into a "blow hole" around Henry's Fork of the Snake River (also possibly known as the Flats) with the entire sled team. It took Lloyd half the night just to get the dogs and sled out, and a few hours more to make his own way out, as every time he went up vertically the wall collapsed even more. Lloyd used his snowshoes for a shovel.

Steve told me by telephone on May 3, 2008 that he wasn't sure if Rex was on that particular run, but this incident is mentioned to show that the mail run wasn't your typical, routine day at the race track, where sled dog teams make five laps around an airplane field covered with snow and one team is declared the winner.

ILLUSTRATION BY BRAD JOHNSON.

The U.S. Mail Run: from the Ward book, page 253:

Some people maintain that dogs do not think but are creatures of habit. Consider this incident. During a mail run from Ashton, Idaho to West Yellowstone Ranger Station, a distance of 64 miles, Lloyd lost the trail in a blizzard. (Author's Note: As an aside, from the Lloyd interview, Lloyd told us he got lost several times in blizzards on the mail run.) After many attempts to find the trail in eight feet of snow, Lloyd told Rex, the lead dog of his all-Samoyed team, to "Go home." Several near disastrous turns and stops later, Rex took off through the forest. (These sudden stops really create tangles in the lines when one is driving a hook-up of 15 dogs.)

Rex began threading his way through the National Forest, leading the team with only a slight pause and cocking of his head now and then as if listening, and the team eventually reached Ashton, Idaho. But they came into town from the south instead of the north as would be usual from Yellowstone. (I) went out with Lloyd several times to take a look at the path which Rex followed into town, but it just didn't make much sense (to us.)

Determined to find out what Rex knew that we didn't, we took him out on a leash and tried the same thing over again. Finally, when off the main traveled path and with repeated commands [of], "Go home," he finally cocked his head, listened, and took off at a trot in the still deep snow.

Thankfully, as we were running behind in deep snow, he stopped and cocked his head as if listening again. This time we listened. We heard the humming and crackling of tiny voices, and realized that the noise was coming from the Forestry Telephone lines laid through the trees, rather than on regular telephone poles.

We were convinced that Rex associated the humming of the lines with people, and by following the sound of the telephone lines into town we duplicated the "new" trail which he created that day.

LLOYD AND REX DELIVERING THE MAIL TO SOME EAGERLY AWAITING CHILDREN.

Lloyd said in his interview that: "(You) don't know where (you) are at, but he (Rex) knows where he is at. They've got a sense of direction that we don't have. Only thing is, if he wants to go that way, why you kind of get in a little bind once in a while...but as soon as they figure it out, (heck) they never get really lost...they get turned around a little. But they're not turned around. Only I'm turned around and confused...."

Mel Fishback wrote in *OWS* that she "went up to Idaho in 1959–60 during the winter and saw the 64 miles that Rex led the mail team on, in continuous runs between Ashton and West Yellowstone, Montana. Mel mentioned that sometimes Lloyd's hound "Red" spelled Rex as Leader on the run. Mel said she has seen what the weather can do along that stretch in the winter. "It took a dog to handle it, and there are few alive that could."

Lloyd told us in the interview that he often had to go back out the same day or in the evening on the mail run, and sometimes took a different team or lead dog to let one team rest. He said he worked them 6 days a week on the mail run. Sometimes it was better to do the run at night on the crusted snow in the moonlight or blizzard.

One time Lloyd was knocked unconscious on the mail run when his sled broke apart and he was hit on the head by a piece of iron bumper from a truck, and his team went 16 miles without him! Rex was at lead this trip. Lloyd said it had been snowing for four days up by the "CC Camp" ("Command Central") at Big Springs, several thousand feet elevation. He said, "The front of his sleigh caught the bumper on a parked or abandoned truck, the sled jack-knifed, slid one corner back, and an iron piece hit me across the nose and conked me out, and those dogs went 8 miles across to Hugginsville and came back.

"When I come to, old Rex was licking me in the face, and I could see this bumper was ripped off of that pickup, and a big old jagged edge and…out there…a little ways…there was mail all over…(heck), (laughs)…you know…but it'd been a 4-day storm and it froze and rained, and drifts.

"When the dogs come back, I straightened the sleigh up as much as I could and…tied across with my anchor rope, and piled that (darn) first class mail. That's all I had was first class mail and two sacks of it. Rex just followed his track…(that he had been on without a driver)."

Later, Lloyd retraced the impromptu "mail run" and was able to retrieve all the mail and could then tell how far the dogs had gone…without him.

After hearing this story, it seems to me like Rex was really "old school"…where he believed that no matter heat, rain, sleet, hail, or snow…"The mail must go through!"…and that it will be delivered—even without a driver! Rex "distributed" the mail on the route, but his technique was surely an unacceptable variance to "standard practice" at the time.

NOTHING DETERS THE DELIVERY OF THE U.S. MAIL,
AS A "TIRED REX" SITTING DOWN IN THE SNOW ATTESTS!
PER KAY KETCHUM, "REX DID DOUBLE-DUTY THAT DAY."
COURTESY KAY KETCHUM.

To help his father sum it up, Steve said in the interview that if the musher dies or get seriously injured on the mail run, he better have the first class mail on his back, his hand clutching pieces of mail in his fist, and be pointed in the direction of the nearest U.S. post office! Lloyd and Steve pretty much were in agreement that they never lost a piece of mail. Sounds like they came close, though, when Lloyd got knocked out by the iron bumper and by default, Rex was "in charge" of the mail run!

CLOSE ENCOUNTER

Another mail run story involved the team meeting up with an aggressive and bold moose on the mail run. It had snowed for 48 days straight. Lloyd had two teams. He had been going in with a slow team in the morning and a fast team at night, which he could let run a bit more to get ready for races. In our interview, he described the incident:

"One day I caught a moose coming onto my trail. He wasn't in sight (of the dogs) when I first seen him, but I couldn't stop the (darn) fool dogs and I broke my brake off trying. We came around the corner...and there he was...and the dogs dove in...and you know they never did that again! This little ace dog, he was swing dog, he popped, whooped around...and the (moose) hit him right on the breast bone and he just slit him like that...16-inch gash right on his chest, just peeled him from his throat back. I sewed him up with some string, he never whimpered either."

From my best estimate, it would appear that Rex may have been just over a year old when he was given a regular role as lead dog on the mail run! He showed he was responsible and could do the job as a leader at an early age. Lloyd thought the other dogs had a lot of respect for Rex. Steve said in the interview that, "The other dogs know he (Rex) is the lead dog...and you are really getting after them (the others) to do what...you're easily telling him (Rex) to do. Rex understood the first time what he was asked to do. He often didn't need to be told, or reminded."

The use of sled dogs to deliver the U.S. mail stopped in this country around 1957.

Perhaps of greatest interest is how Rex got his name. Gaines Dog Food Company asked Lloyd to identify a great sled dog and to explain what it takes to make a great sled dog. As it was reported by several others in the sport of sledding, sometimes one mile per hour in the snow was a good speed, as the Leader had to break trail, and the snow was higher than the dog's withers before the dog could hit the bottom of the trail and rise up again to move forward! This picture shows Lloyd in action with Rex during a training session.

CHAPTER 7

REX, *THE BLIZZARD KING!*

How Rex Got His Name:
"The Blizzard King!"

From an undated *WKW* issue, circa 1953/4: Vera Lawrence wrote:

"Of particular interest to our readers will be the news that Mr. Harry Miller, Director of the Gaines Research Center had written a letter to Mr. Van Sickle, requesting: 'Out of the wealth of your knowledge and experience with sled dogs could you answer a question put to us by one of the big magazines?' The inquirers were interested in having a sled dog, either living or in the past, who could be rated as a Dog Great to go alongside outstanding sheepdog, bloodhound, greyhound, etc.

"Mr. Van Sickle's letter, in reply to Mr. Miller's request for facts and reasons for his choice is of such interest it rates publication in full, as follows:

"Dear Mr. Miller:

I feel honored that you consider me as qualified to make a choice of a great sled dog. It is the most difficult decision that I have ever had to make. You see, a sled dog team is comparable to a football team. While one player is a good quarterback, he would make a poor tackle. Also, one dog may be a good "wheeler" but a poor "leader" and still be a good sled dog. But since a good lead dog is most indispensable I will first limit the field to lead dogs.

(1)—My ideal lead dog must have the following qualities: The ability to hold the towline tight at all times. He must get the feel of it and pick up any slack instantly. He must be able to make a "Comeback" "Haw"—straight back and still keep the towline straight.

2)—He must have a sense of responsibility. It has been my experience that some dogs are born with it and they are the only ones that you can train into a good leader.

(3)—Power and Strength; (4) Endurance; (5) Speed; (6) Adaptability; (7) Versatility.

I have been training dogs for twenty years and the lead dog that comes nearer to filling those qualifications is a Samoyed Lead Dog owned by Mrs. A. E. Mason of Sacramento, California, that I have been training and working since he was nine months old. His name is registered Rex of White Way—I prefer to call him The Blizzard King. He is not quite three years old but has the qualities usually possessed by leaders 8 and 9 years old.

In February of this year, a plane developed engine trouble, flying from Sacramento to Reno and crashed up on the snow bound emergency Truckee Airport. They called me to attempt to go in with the dogs. I started out at 10:00 o'clock at night in pitch dark and it was 18 degrees below zero. I hooked 18 dogs up and towed two sleds and Ed Crandall went with me. There was generally no trail and I just had a general idea of the direction to go. But I put Rex on lead and since he has that most important quality of keeping the towline tight we made it to there in good time without any entanglements although I couldn't see the dogs.

Then I loaded the most injured man on one sled and hooked my seven Targhee speed dogs on one sled and started back to the waiting ambulance. I lent seven Samoyed dogs with "Rex" on lead for Ed Crandall to drive out and bring the other three men. They made it back in good time. Since Ed Crandall had never driven a dog team before, about all he did was hang on, and Rex brought them out, proving his sense of responsibility.

He is equally good on slow heavy pulling that requires endurance, or on light fast going, as in a race, that requires speed.

He is the best dog I have ever known to break trail in virgin snow. Also, he is the best dog I have ever seen to be able to face into a fierce blizzard and keep going. This I believe is due to his slanted eyes and heavy lashes that permit him to see where other dogs are forced to turn their heads.

He is the most versatile lead dog I have ever seen. Before I had him, I usually had one dog that would break virgin snow and still another for a race and perhaps another for exhibition or parade work, but Rex is good for any of it.

He is most happy when breaking a trail in virgin snow, but he performs his lead dog duties equally well, pulling a sled on wheels in an arena before 10,000 people, as he did recently in the Western Sportsman's show at the Los Angeles Gilmore Stadium.

I had a special lead dog that I had trained since 1942 to use just for exhibition and parades. He got hurt so I had to use another. I tried Rex and he did as well the first time as the tenth.

So my decision is that Rex "The Blizzard King" is qualified to be rated as a Great Sled Dog.

Yours very truly,
Lloyd Van Sickle"

LLOYD, WITH REX LEADING THE TEAM DOWN
THE PRECARIOUS MOUNTAINSIDE,
AT THE RESCUE OF THE *CITY OF SAN FRANCISCO* PASSENGER TRAIN.
ORIGINAL ART BY NAN HOLT, "RESCUE AT YUBA GAP,"
WINNER, "BEST IN ART SHOW," SCA 2012 NATIONAL.
PHOTOGRAPH BY NEIL KOPPES. COURTESY NAN HOLT.

CHAPTER 8

"HIGH SIERRA MOUNTAINS RESCUE 1952"

THE MODERN-DAY DONNER PARTY ABOARD *CITY OF SAN FRANCISCO* PASSENGER TRAIN AT DONNER PASS

As A Backdrop...

Around the country in 1952, Puerto Rico was proclaimed a Commonwealth on July 25. Richard Nixon, as Vice-Presidential candidate, gave his "Checker's Speech," so called because of his sentimental reference to his dog "Checkers" on September 23. In Southern California, the filming was wrapping up on one of Hollywood's greatest musicals, *Singin' in the Rain*, with Gene Kelly, Debbie Reynolds, Cyd Charisse, and Donald O'Conner.

The Snow Storm of the Century!

At a much higher elevation in the High Sierras, they weren't in a singing frame of mind, as the precipitation came down in the form of small white ice crystals, that just kept on coming.

As was reported in numerous sources following the momentous event that was to come, Rex, *The Blizzard King* picked the *blizzard of the century* up at Yuba Gap/Donner Pass near Truckee, California to go down in history...and showed that it takes more than a man, or many men, to get the job done!

THIS IS THE "LANDSCAPE" CREATED BY THE MOMENTOUS BLIZZARD!
NO WONDER IT WAS CALLED "THE BLIZZARD OF THE CENTURY."
COURTESY NEVADA HISTORICAL SOCIETY.

As Jim Cheskawich observed (and Sheila Goffe, Breed Columns Editor, affirmed in the *AKC Gazette* in February 2008):

This was no publicity stunt for the media and no Academy Awards were given out, but this was serious work involving 226 passengers and crew stranded aboard [a] luxury streamliner. Even though nearly 1,000 people were involved in the massive rescue effort from several states and using different means of transportation to reach the train, they needed *"The Blizzard King"* because he had a special role to deliver Dr. Lawrence D. Nelson by dogsled."

There was only one dog that could guarantee mission accomplishment under these difficult circumstances: the purebred Samoyed known as "The Blizzard King."

THE *CITY OF SAN FRANCISCO* PASSENGER TRAIN
TRAPPED ON THE MOUNTAINSIDE AT DONNER PASS SUMMIT,
NEAR YUBA GAP, JANUARY 13, 1952.
COURTESY NEVADA HISTORICAL SOCIETY.

CITY OF SAN FRANCISCO TRAIN RESCUE

Alice Thompson Lombardi was a friend of Agnes Mason's and remembered Rex at the Golden Gate Show in January of 1952. Alice was 12 years old when she was working as an assistant to the show photographer, Gene Bennett, when Rex had to get permission to leave the bench show to help out with the stranded *City of San Francisco* train. Alice said in the interview with her in March 2004 that she followed the judge or the Superintendent who marked off the catalogue as dogs were excused for the rescue, and it was a two-day show. Alice thought that Aljean helped transport Rex and other White Way Samoyeds to Lloyd for the rescue.

Aljean reported in a *Samoyed Quarterly* interview that Rex and the dog team were needed to take the doctor to the train. "There was no food available, no medical supplies, and diesel fuel for heating was running out—up at the stranded train."

AN AERIAL VIEW OF THE TRAIN TRAPPED ON THE MOUNTAINSIDE.
COURTESY NEVADA HISTORICAL SOCIETY.

As Sheila Goffe wrote in the February 28, 2008 issue of *The American Kennel Club (AKC) Gazette:*

"The only hope appeared to be dogsled. Southern Pacific called on Lloyd Van Sickle, one of the top drivers in the country. The only problem was that his leader, the *"Blizzard King"* was at a dog show in San Francisco, hundreds of miles away. He was preparing for his turn in the ring. He didn't show much but here was a chance for that elusive major. It was a bench show, which meant he was supposed to stay at the show all day."

Lloyd said in his interview with us that Dr. Nelson (who also made many other rescues with Lloyd and Rex and knew the routine), was told to *just hold on tight* as they approached the stranded train. "I told him to get a hold of the slats in the bottom before I get there and he (asked) what's that for? I said just hang on, don't move your feet…and hook your toe on that (gosh darn) rope and just rear back and keep your mouth shut. Well, we went down there and…I just laid her (sled) on her side and put the rudders right up on them cars…and I managed to keep her on that. It was bumpy but we made it."

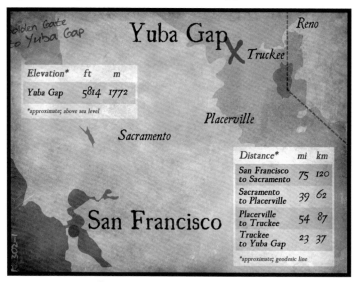

ILLUSTRATION BY BRAD JOHNSON.

REX FACES AN *AVALANCHE* POSSIBILITY!

It appears that after Rex was flown from San Francisco to join up with Lloyd at Truckee, he and other dogs were placed on a working westbound train car at Truckee to be transported as close as possible to the stranded train—which had been sitting up in the mountains for a few days. Then when the working train could get no closer on an open track, Rex, Lloyd, and the sled dog team were sent on their rescue by dog sled with Dr. Nelson.

Lloyd said he worked just as hard as the dogs worked.

Lloyd said that they had to worry about sliding, locking up the sled, and causing an AVALANCHE, which would have sent the entire train into the ravine below! Lloyd said the train was hanging on the bluff. An avalanche was a real fear which could send the train hurtling down the mountain side into the ravine below!

Although snow-sheds and state of the art snow removal equipment were available, no one anticipated the "Pride of the Fleet" getting stuck in about 13 feet of snow with drifting creating packed snow at higher levels up to 26 feet.

Rex and Lloyd had to navigate carefully as they approached the train so they wouldn't set off an avalanche or go over the mountain's edge with the sled team, driver, and Dr. Nelson!

Several trains and rescue cars had passed by on the parallel track even after the train got stuck, but everyone that passed by without stopping, thought *someone else* would take care of the problem. By the time Rex showed up, one crew member and a rescuer had died from overexertion or avalanche, respectively. There was no heat inside the train and the passengers had tied bed sheets and layers of newspapers around their legs and arms to stay warm.

Some of the elderly passengers needed medical evaluations to ascertain any serious problems.

The dogsled was put on its side to keep from going over a cliff and to slow its downward approach to the train. Otherwise, it was going into the ravine below...and *could have taken the train with it with an avalanche!*

As in a war zone, there is usually something happening around the clock and it is impossible to track everything of importance that occurs. Eyewitnesses usually provide their observations later and slowly a "story" emerges. What happened at one end of the train concerning new information, hazards, rescue efforts, etc. was difficult to communicate to the other end. People probably alternately panicked, cried, and prayed. Some got off the train, wandered around, and may have gotten disoriented for a time.

THE *CITY OF SAN FRANCISCO* ENCASED IN SNOW.
COURTESY NEVADA HISTORICAL SOCIETY.

Rex performed admirably on the slow but careful approach to the train and, as Lloyd said, seemed to act as if he knew this was an important, and historically significant, rescue.

This was a very special mission and Rex played his part in an event that would be remembered forever in the lore of Donner Pass, Southern Pacific Railroad, and great blizzards! This was no ordinary rescue effort and it took many players, hours, and resources.

Author's Note:

For those interested in further research, *Snowbound Streamliner, Rescuing the 1952 City of San Francisco* by Robert J. Church, Signature Press 2000, provides detailed hourly activities, spanning several days, for the time period preceding, during, and following the rescue of the "Pride of the Fleet." Dog teams are mentioned in several places in the book as providing assistance. Page 78 and 79 record: "Then it was learned that rotary 7210's pusher engine, AC 4173, had derailed its truck at MP 187 (1.5 miles east of Troy) and was stalled. It was decided to send Dr. Nelson to '101' by dog sled." No. 101 refers to the *City of San Francisco.*

Page 79 further records: "... Jay Gold and Charles Swing...met the dog sled teams around 2:00 p.m. The doctor and two other men were breaking trail for the dogs whose heads were barely [visible] above the snow. It was just after 4:00 p.m. when they got Dr. Nelson and more food aboard the train. About 40 were in the elderly class, and Dr. Nelson examined them all. He determined that none were in too bad a condition considering the circumstances."

Mark McLaughlin is an author who is known as "The Storm King" and he writes about the Lake Tahoe, Sierra Nevada, Truckee, and Reno areas. Mark has been instrumental in helping to bring the Rex story to life, both for the book and for the docu-drama. He reported on his website (www.thestormking.com/donner.pdf) that a morphine addict on the train was going through withdrawal episodes and acting out. He was locked in his compartment for a period and was a potentially serious problem. It was reported elsewhere that he did make it to the end of the trip (Sacramento) without apparent damage or harm to himself, the train, or others.

Per Mark, there were 226 passengers involved in the stranded train along with a full complement of crew members. Dr. Nelson provided needed medical supplies and treatment for the injured passengers and crew members.

ENGINE 101, THE PRIDE OF THE FLEET

The *City of San Francisco,* Engine 101, was the pride of the fleet. In some ways what happened to this train was reminiscent to some of the *Titanic*, which also was considered the best ocean going vessel of its time. However, unlike the *Titanic*, all the passengers aboard the train were rescued.

About the famous train rescue, Mel Fishbank thought Rex was spelled by two different dogs. "Any dog that could take part of responsibility was a good dog." Mel hated to see Rex's accomplishments dulled by the sort of bragging that makes it impossible for the dog to have been real. "The snow was soft and wet, the trail breaking all uphill. It was all good dogs that made the trip; the average Sam wouldn't have made it."

In the phone interview with Lloyd back in March 2004, I asked Lloyd about the lead dog(s) used on the train rescue. Lloyd confirmed that Rex and Red (the great Targhee Hound) had to be spelled off at Lead, as the trail consisted of a few inches of snow mixed with mud, and the pull was sometimes uphill to the rescue site. "The trail was many miles in snow, shrubs, bushes, and mud on sled and uphill. It was quite a pull."

MAN'S BEST FRIEND

Alice Lombardi told me in her interview that there was a story going around after the rescue that the White Way team, with Rex as Leader, *refused* to leave the train site after delivering the doctor and medical supplies. There was a man who had apparently fallen into a crevice and had disappeared from view. However, the White Way Samoyeds sensed that the man was still alive and balked at leaving until the man was pulled up to safety!

Alice said the man had apparently wandered, gotten lost, and fell out of sight. Alice said she never saw this written up and doesn't remember much more. She also offered that some things about Rex were possibly embellished, but can't be proven or disproved any longer.

REX, *"The Blizzard King"*

In conclusion, according to Mark McLaughlin's write-up on his website: "The critical rescue mission had taken four days and cost two lives, but all 226 passengers and crew were eventually saved. From January 10 to 17, nearly 13 feet of snow fell. The winter of 1951–52 dumped 65 feet of snow on Donner Summit and the snowpack reached 26-feet deep, the greatest depth ever recorded there."

So, yes indeed, Rex really did pick the "Blizzard of the Century" to affirm his nickname of *"The Blizzard King."*

THE PRICE OF BEING A "HERO"

As with the momentous *City of San Francisco* rescue, when Rex got taken off a "benched show" to go to work, he couldn't use his accumulated sick leave, annual leave, "credit hours," or vacation time to beg off. A lot of effort and expense were put into obtaining his services to fly him up to Truckee, California from San Francisco. He had to be 100% reliable each time the call came for him to help.

In this case, with snow piling up 20–30 feet deep and with drifting and wind gusts close to 90 miles-per-hour up at the Yuba Gap, *The Blizzard King* could have just as easily been transported back to Siberia, working through the elements like his ancestors from several thousand years ago. Rex was in top physical condition and a superb athlete. His ancestors had been bred to do this kind of work as a way of life to support and help mankind survive. It was in his genes.

Rex made history that day by foregoing the chance for that elusive "major" that would have added "Ch." as the prefix to his registered kennel name. But to the 226 passengers and crew on the *City of San Francisco* he certainly was their "Champion"...and a hero for all of us.

THE TRAIN, AND ITS PASSENGERS,
COULD HAVE TUMBLED INTO THE DEEP RAVINE, SEEN AT THE LEFT.
INSTEAD... THEY WERE SAVED!
COURTESY NEVADA HISTORICAL SOCIETY.

20   D   Oakland Tribune, Thursday, Jan. 17, 1952

DRAMA IN THE SIERRA

Tribune aerial photo by Donnie Wilson from plane flown by Tommy Sheridan

The Southern Pacific streamliner City of San Francisco lies buried under mountainous snows on the slopes of the High Sierra near Yuba Gap. This exclusive photo was taken shortly before rescue parties reached the train yesterday. Head of the train is at bottom right of photo.

January 1952
(By Mark McLaughlin/Edited by Steve Brandt)

Fifty-five years ago, a major blizzard shut down Interstate 40 (precursor to I-80) for 30 days straight. Not only was the vital transcontinental highway closed for a month, but a luxury train was stopped cold in the mountains with 226 passengers and crew onboard. The event was major news at the time.

The *City of San Francisco* was the pride of the Southern Pacific train fleet. At its inauguration on January 2, 1938, the state-of-the-art passenger train was deemed the "world's most superlative train." She consisted of deluxe sleepers and coaches loaded with amenities, and she had motive power supplied by six 900-horsepower engines. A technological marvel in engineering, the train was proclaimed "the largest, fastest, most beautiful, powerful, and luxurious streamliner ever designed." (The description reminded one of the "unsinkable" luxury ocean liner, *Titanic* of 1912!)

The elegant $2 million train took transcontinental travel to a whole new level in terms of speed and comfort. It made five round trips each month between Oakland and Chicago, hurtling the distance between the Windy City and the Golden Gate in less than 40 hours at speeds exceeding 100 mph.

The Fateful Day

On Sunday, January 13, 1952, the *City of San Francisco* rammed into a deep snow slide east of Yuba Gap, about 20 miles west of Donner Pass. When engineers put the train into reverse to escape, the steel wheels slipped on the icy track. Nobody panicked. After all, the luxury train was more powerful and better equipped than any other train on the line. Among the 196 travelers on board were representatives bound for a Republican National Committee meeting in San Francisco and soldiers bound for the Korean War. No one really expected to be stopped by a mere snow slide very long.

Hours Pass

However, the passengers' laissez-faire attitude turned slowly to anger when they were still snowbound 24 hours later.

The wind was fierce, howling at speeds in excess of 90 mph and snow drifts towered 20 to 30 feet outside the frosty windows. Many feared it would be just a matter of time before another avalanche would shove the entire train into the steep ravine next to the train. Mid-day Monday, 30 hours into the ordeal and no rescue in sight, the supply of diesel fuel ran out. When the power quit, the passenger compartments were pitched into a cold, eerie darkness.

Rescue Parties

Even as the blizzard raged on, SP rescue trains were inching their way closer from both east and west toward the stranded streamliner. One train carried dogsled teams. The Sixth Army trucked in Weasels (over-snow track vehicles) and soldiers trained in winter survival. Military doctors and nurses were rushed to likely rescue points near the stranded train. During a brief lull in the storm, a Coast Guard helicopter managed to drop medical supplies and food.

At one point, an avalanche struck a rotary snowplow (also scheduled to be in the Truckee Railroad Museum) manned by engineer Rolland Raymond of Sacramento and he was killed. Another rescuer, 36-year-old Jay Gold, died of a heart attack from his exertions.

Storm Stops (Finally)

When the deadly storm broke on January 16, relief parties rushed in for the rescue. The cold and weary passengers hobbled to safety along the tracks while the sick and weak were tobogganed or carried on stretchers. Miraculously, all 226 passengers and crew survived their three-day ordeal on the snowbound train.

Record Blizzard

Nearly 13 feet of snow had blasted the region that week. The storm of January 1952 dumped nearly 65 feet of snow on Donner Summit and the snow pack itself reached 26 feet deep, the greatest depth ever recorded there. [NOTE: 65 feet of snow was the snowfall accumulation measured for the whole winter.]

CALIFORNIA CREWS EMPLOYED POWERFUL SNOWBLOWERS TO CLEAR HIGHWAY 40
AFTER THE BLIZZARD OF 1952, BUT THE VITAL ROUTE
REMAINED IMPASSABLE FOR 30 DAYS STRAIGHT.
PHOTOGRAPH BY ROBERT GERDEL.
COURTESY MARK MCLAUGHLIN/GERDEL COLLECTION.

**THIS WAS TAKEN AT LONG BEACH.
REX IS IN ON THE RIGHT, HANDLED BY ALJEAN MASON.**

CHAPTER 9

REX: THE MIDDLE YEARS
1952–1956

As A Backdrop...

As Rex turned 6 years old, the following was going on in 1952: The first hydrogen bomb was exploded November 1 in the Pacific. Boxer Rocky Marciano became Heavy Weight Champion. Polio vaccine was invented by Jonas Salk. In 1953, the Rosenbergs were convicted of "conspiracy" and were executed in the Sing Sing Prison's "electric chair." The Korean War armistice was signed July 27. Crick and Watson unveiled their famous double helix model of DNA. Rhythm and Blues (R&B) innovators, Hank Ballard and the Midnighters, cut their first recording. *Shane* and *From Here to Eternity* are on the screen. Princess Elizabeth is crowned Queen of England. Sir Edmund Hillary and Tenzing Norgay ascended the summit of Mt. Everest. And the Corvette automobile goes on sale.

1952: THE SAN MATEO HOOKUP

From interviews, it was noted that Rex once had 60 dogs hitched up behind him! No actual written accounts remain as to the date, place, or purpose. Lloyd possibly did it on a bet, or because it hadn't been done before. There are, however, several very reliable written reports of a 25-dog team hookup in San Mateo, California with our Rex as Leader. This occurred at the site of the Samoyed Club of America National Specialty. Almost 30% of the Samoyeds at the 1952 National Specialty were involved in the hookup, which speaks very well for the breed.

From the November and December 1952 *WKW*:

This group at San Mateo was made up of all of the dogs, including the leaders of the five teams that competed in the exhibition race that day. Their combined efforts with the Mason veteran lead dog, Rex of White Way, with Lloyd Van Sickle in charge, got that car on the move (a full sized Ford convertible). Moreover, in spite of the various kennels that these dogs represented and with different leaders there was complete harmony among them, thus enabling the trainers to put on a satisfactory exhibit which was entirely unrehearsed.

This was a never to be forgotten thrill for all who saw or took part in it. The race was easily won by the Mason team of 4 trained dogs. Team 1-Driver, Lloyd Van Sickle, Led by Rex of White Way. Others in team: Ch. White Way's Silver Streak, Ch. Trooperine of White Way (b), and White Way Jacko.

Rex was the Leader of the winning team at the San Mateo Kennel Club Show and Leader of the 25 dog (all Samoyeds) Team Exhibition Hookup, San Mateo, California.

From the *SCA Bulletin*, Summer 1952 on the same event:

On commands, given by Lloyd Van Sickle, the remarkable Rex worked the whole group back and forth across the track to give the numerous photographers some good action shots. The dogs all seemed to enjoy the experience as much as the spectators.... A specially selected team of 15 was chosen for a demonstration for television and motion picture cameras. This team, led by Rex of White Way and including eight show champions, coursed the mile track, executing right and left turns and complete about turns.

In a follow-up 1952 Letter of Appreciation to SCA Members regarding "The Dog World Award for Outstanding Service to Dogs" presented to Agnes Mason at San Mateo, Mrs. Mason wrote for the *SCA Bulletin* how she started in training a team:

After 18 years of owning Sams, we thrilled at seeing the exhibition put on by the 5 teams at San Mateo. It was an experience never to be forgotten. To receive the award you presented me, and then to see this demonstration in conclusion, was most gratifying. Even though we cannot carry on this special promotion as extensively as we have in the past, we feel many others will become enthused to the extent that they will continue the interest and activity now stimulated. No one could wish for better results. I thank you one and all.

Always,

A friend in breed, Agnes Mason.

1952: "SHOWTIME!"

Rex was 6 years-of-age when he was entered in the Reno Show and won "Winners Dog" and "Best of Winners." In today's Samoyed Conformation Ring, most of the Samoyeds are "finished" with their show career and even the "specials" have made their mark on the breed by this point. However, this is a slow developing breed and the good ones, like Rex, will hold up and compete successfully and can win Regional and National Specialties even into their second decade.

Alice Lombardi said in the 2004 interview that Rex "was built like a truck, and spoiled rotten by Agnes and Aljean and any other women visiting or in residence at the Mason household."

She added, "At shows under male judges, Rex was all business. But...for female judges...he was an imp. If he thought the judge didn't like him, Rex knew this and started raising his paw as if to beg, or cocked his head to look cute and stand out."

Alice said emphatically that Rex was not trained to do this but knew he was in there to win and this was part of his arsenal of tricks. Alice went on to say that Agnes believed that Rex could do anything. "He sang and played the piano. He was spoiled and obviously was Agnes's favorite Samoyed. He was treated like a human being."

Agnes Mason's granddaughter, Sandie Flettner, relayed to me in a telephone conversation in September 2012 that Rex not only "played" the piano, but he also "sang," too! She lived with the Masons for a while and saw Rex in action. She adds that Agnes "kept the sessions short," so that Rex wouldn't damage his eardrums from the loud singing.

**SANDIE FLETTNER AND AGNES MASON
WITH A BELOVED SAMOYED OF WHITE WAY KENNELS.
COURTESY SANDIE FLETTNER.**

1953: WEST YELLOWSTONE DOG DERBY

With no rescue work to keep them away, Rex and Lloyd left Truckee, California to attend the "West Yellowstone Dog Derby" in Montana. Lloyd took along his Targhee Hounds, as well as members of the Mason White Way Samoyed team. The Van Sickle brothers (Lloyd and Bob) had a pet bear in their team, but it had no patience with the dogs if they were slow and would speed them up with a swipe of its paw.

As was reported in the *Western Kennel World* (*WKW*) in early spring of 1953, Rex was the Leader of Lloyd's Targhee Hounds and won the West Yellowstone Dog Derby in Montana on February 22, 1953. He won the speed race and later the draft race with all Samoyeds. It was said that before the speed race started, comments were heard to the effect that "Lloyd can't win the speed race with that white dog out there!" Rex may not have started out as fast as some of the other dogs that were his competitors, but he did most of the pulling on his team. *WKW* wrote that the winning time in the speed race was "12 miles, 60 minutes."

Lloyd told us in the interview that he put Rex in back on the right side, which is the hardest position. He said that's one of the two dogs you can't get rid of because they become too attached to you—the right wheeler and the Leader."

Rex also ran on the team with his kennel mate Jacko in the Freight Team Race and won that pulling 315 pounds! A dog named Lucky, who was a Targhee Hound, was the lead dog in both of these races on the same date. Lucky was not a Samoyed, but Rex worked on his team for the speed as well as the freight races. In the speed race, Rex ended up doing most of the pulling to enable the team to win. His kennel mate Jacko presumably did his share of the pulling in the freight race so Rex didn't have to carry another team on the same day.

LLOYD, WITH REX AND THE TEAM AT YELLOWSTONE. REX IS TO THE RIGHT WITH HIS TONGUE HANGING OUT! LUCKY IS THE DOG TO THE LEFT.

1953–1954: Other Achievements

During the time period spanning 1953-1954, Rex also worked as Leader of a dog sled team pulling 600-pound loads of wood to repair Donner Lake piers in a winter emergency. Evidence of Rex's labor probably still survives today. According to Steve Van Sickle, no plaque or memorial is in place indicating that Rex brought the loads in. Steve thought that Lloyd and Rex brought in half the Donner Lake piers for the boat docks. Those two also hauled piers into Tahoe in the winter time when the sap was low, and the trees could be cut easier and didn't weigh as much.

Rex also worked as Leader of the dog sled team hauling Christmas Trees on the 34-mile roundtrip, daily run. The assignment possibly lasted several weeks or more, over several seasons, and Rex helped haul in the Christmas trees for commercial sales. Lloyd cut the trees and used the dogs to haul them out of the woods, same as he did for the logging when he did the work for Donner Lake.

THIS WAS A TROPHY PROVIDED BY KAREN SICKLE OF NEW YORK,
WITH ARTWORK BY KAREN SICKLE,
IN HONOR OF REBEL, OWNED BY JIM CHESKAWICH,
WHO PLACED AT THE SAMOYED CLUB OF AMERICA WEIGHT-PULL CONTEST IN 1997.
PHOTOGRAPH BY NOEL JOHNSON. COURTESY JIM CHESKAWICH.

In 1954, here are some activities around the nation: Nautilus, the first atomic-powered submarine, was launched at Groton, Connecticut January 21. The U.S. Senate voted to condemn Senator Joseph McCarthy (R-Wisconsin) for his abuse of the senate during anti-Communist hearings and debates. The U.S. Supreme Court ruled unanimously May 17 that racial segregation in public schools was unconstitutional, in Brown v. Board of Education of Topeka. Ernest Hemingway won the Nobel Prize in literature for *Old Man and the Sea*, Elvis Presley cut his first record, and Marlon Brando was starring in *On the Waterfront.* "Rock Around the Clock" by Bill Hailey and the Comets is a popular song.

1954: "REX SETS A WORLD RECORD!"

The following "West Yellowstone Weight Pulling Contest" is from the Gertrude Adams' files and shows Rex's versatility and his "World Class" strength: "Rex broke the World Record for weight pulling at a contest in West Yellowstone, Montana on February 22, 1954. At age 7, Rex weighed 70 pounds and pulled 1,870 pounds—an average pull of 26.7 pounds per pound of body weight. This beat the Alaska record and also set the World Record."

Lloyd told us in the phone interview in 2004: "The pull was on freezing rain and ice. If the pull wasn't made in 30 seconds, the runners on the sled would ice up, making the pull much more difficult, if not impossible. But Rex had a technique for making the weight pull. After I hauled him over, he'd make a run, and hit that sucker and it'd break loose, and then he'd dig in and pull it. If he stopped, it'd freeze down and you were done for...so it was a little skill."

Lloyd also told us in the 2004 interview that Rex was sick the night before the weight pull, and he planned to have Rex make just one pull unless he had to do more. He told Al Holden, who was another weight-pull competitor who was working with a Malmute named Tobe, that if Tobe got eliminated, Lloyd wouldn't have to use Rex again. Lloyd said, "I'll tell you what I'll do... I'll pull Rex once, and then if Tobe's still a'pulling, I'll take Rex and pull him against you."

Rex did set the new World Record that day for all dogs... all breeds ... as pound-for-pound he showed that he could out-pull anyone!

As a side note, it is interesting that 50 years after Wilt Chamberlin scored 100 points in a NBA basketball game on March 2, 1962, we find out from a special televised commemorative documentary that Wilt didn't sleep at all the night before he set his own record!

REX, OUR LEAD DOG WITH LLOYD VANSICKLE

FEB. 22, 1954

REX OF WHITEWAY

Broke the world's record in a pulling contest in West Yellowstone.

Pulled Alone, 1870 lbs.

5 other breeds of dogs competing.

MASON'S WHITEWAY KENNELS

RT. 7, BOX 3483   SACRAMENTO, CALIF.

COURTESY CAROL CHITTUM.

A.E. Mason Passes on December 6, 1954

Agnes' husband passed away in 1954. He had been ill for some time. The A.E. Mason Memorial Trophy was created and offered to the Samoyed attaining the most points for Best of Breed wins, Group Placings, or Best in Show.

While the Trophy is no longer given out,
A. E. Mason's love—and appreciation—for the Samoyed breed
is reflected in this tribute medal.
Photograph by Noel Johnson.
Courtesy Jim and Celinda Cheskawich.

As A Backdrop...

In 1955, the U.S. agreed to help train the South Vietnamese army. The Supreme Court ordered "All deliberate speed" in integration of public schools, May 31. Rosa Parks refused on December 1 to give her seat to a white man on a bus in Montgomery, Alabama. Her arrest, detention, and conviction sparked a boycott of the bus system by Rev. Martin Luther King, Jr. and bus segregation was declared unconstitutional by federal court in 1956. America's two largest labor organizations merged December 5, creating AFL-CIO. Coca Cola was now sold in cans. "Disneyland" opened in California on July 17. James Dean starred in *East of Eden* and *Rebel Without a Cause.*

In 1956, the Federal-Aid Highway Act was signed June 29, creating the Interstate Highway System. The first transatlantic cable was activated on September 25. On October 8, in game 5, Don Larsen pitched the only perfect World Series game. Eugene O'Neill's *Long Day's Journey into Night* opened in November on Broadway, *High Society* is on the screen with Grace Kelly, and *My Fair Lady* opened Broadway. Patsy Cline records "Walkin' After Midnight."

1956: "BIG BEAR RACES"

From the March 1956 *WKW*:

The Big Bear Valley Sled Dog Derby (So. Cal) was held February 5, 1956. The Sammies took the day as every event was won by a Samoyed team. Third place in the two and a half mile race was won by Lloyd Van Sickle with his three dog team led by Rex of White Way. The weight pulling contest was won by the team led by Rex of White Way.

As Agnes was quoted in the *WKW* write-up:

Lloyd did not know about the races until a few days before when he came down to help me fix up some kennels, therefore, Jacko and Rex were not conditioned for a long race—but Lloyd became enthused about entering Rex in the pulling event—as I did too. We took the dogs thinking we might help fill in some team for certain events.

Naturally we are happy that Rex won the pulling match …(And) we were also happy that Rex and his three teammates, Blizzard, Blazer, and Jacko, won the sprint race of 350 yards in 30 seconds.... *Another proof that show dogs can be work dogs as well.* [Emphasis added!]

Lloyd and I enjoyed the events and do wish the Southern California members much success for bigger and better races. With patience and endurance, Big Bear can be a noted place for racing and other events. It is a good place for young future mushers to practice for future winners—and should be encouraged for the sport as well as to win.

Mush! Downtown Goes to the Dogs...

It was tough sledding in San Francisco today. Why? Heh, heh, heh—no snow, of course. But that didn't deter Lloyd Van Sickle and his dog team from sledding through the downtown district to publicize the March of Dimes and the Sierra Nevada Dog Derby at Truckee Feb. 10-12.

WHETHER IT WAS BIG BEAR, OR TRUCKEE, OR DOWNTOWN SAN FRANCISCO,
REX WAS ALWAYS READY TO LEAD!

Rex, showcasing his "long legs," making him...
"Able to go through windows in a single leap!"

CHAPTER 10

"A FORCE OF NATURE"

Lloyd said he could depend on Rex for anything—tied, or loose, whether in harness or not. However... "Rex did have a sense of humor!"

REX "ON THE RUN"

From the interview, Lloyd recounted that at one time he had the team on a big ranch back behind Truckee. They were with an insurance representative and a fellow from the Forest Service. They had been up there the day before with a full load of saws as there was building damage from the heavy snowfall. Lloyd anchored the team to a good root off of one of the pines and both men in the sled. "I reached back and got the anchor rope and when I did they (the sled team) all saw me. I jerked it and it caught something that the loop didn't go through and that snap whistled past my ear and broke that big snap that was hooked on the sleigh and away they went. No words I could yell loud enough...could turn them back and so I took off after them...17 miles out there I run that sucker! I could just about catch them, but he (Rex) seemed like he was going in those downhills...and I was just about at the same speed that he (Rex) drove, in the day before, all with a load up.

"I got in there...he'd made the loop. I followed his track right around and there he was...just... laying on the snow and every dog laying in their position where I'd left them all day while (others) shoveled snow. There was nothing I could make a sled out of. Finally I found a 2 by 6 about 3 feet long.

"I got a rope around it some way, the anchor rope, and I got partly ridden (back) down."

A "High-Jumper!"

Once in a stadium at one of Rex' numerous "dog and pony" shows, the assistants were supposed to quickly put away the many 2½-foot gates that the "ponies" had jumped in succession, before Rex was called in to work. When the call came for Rex to come out with Lloyd, Rex took the White Way team over the 2½-foot-high wooden jumps (all dogs following in harness and gangline!) and Lloyd had to heave the sled over each of the jumps...without disrupting the team's momentum. Lloyd told us in the interview that everyone thought it was part of the act!

Lloyd did tell me that "Rex would climb a tree...if I asked him."

A "Travelin' Dog"

Alice Lombardi told me a story about an "incident" she witnessed at a motel when Agnes was traveling with several female companions. Agnes had left the bathroom window open as she always did for Rex. At some point well after midnight Rex jumped through the open window to relieve himself from boredom and to take his nightly walk by himself. The sound of banging garbage cans and lids and rolling bottles served to awaken one of the ladies, who immediately screamed out that it was her own female Samoyed that had escaped and they all had to help her find her Samoyed. Another lady in the traveling group remarked that it was "only Rex taking his nightly walk," and there was nothing we could, or should, do about it and we need to get back to sleep. It appears that Rex never ran out to the roadway, although they sometimes stayed near highways in motels.

Agnes had discovered earlier that it was better to be awakened by garbage cans then by smashed windows, whenever Rex was in the room. Rex used to go through windows routinely, even at the Mason's home. When it was time to leave a hotel early in the morning and drive to the dog show site, no one wants to be delayed to have a room inspection to count broken windows!

"As Aljean said, 'Rex is a clever thinker is proved by his ability to obtain his desires. For one thing, Rex hates fences—he will jump any fence, scale them with little trouble. He will tear down or go through any windows to call upon a *special* Sammy girl. He has learned how to open the double-hung windows—with never a tell-tale tooth mark on the window sill either.'

"Aljean caught Rex going through a window once at home, and made him go back inside using the same window. Usually, Agnes and Aljean left the windows open about a-foot-high for Rex at home or at hotels, as Rex was going to jump through—with or without the glass in place—and no amount of training or retraining was going to change him!"

A "STUBBORN DOG"...ONCE

Lloyd said in his 2004 interview that there was only one time when Rex balked. A friend, Rudy Dawson, had asked Lloyd to come down to a football game to put on an exhibition with Rex during half-time. Rex became frightened by a Frankenstein balloon and wouldn't go down the steps. To entice Rex, Lloyd hooked up a puppy named "Ted" who proceeded to run around madly and act like he was going to eat that balloon character.

Lloyd spoke calmly to Rex, and he went out and made his half-circle and then plopped the whole team down. Lloyd said the team was never trained to lie down in harness, but "it was hot, they were tired, and their tongues were hanging out." Lloyd said that Rex made a perfect exhibition, and on the way back Lloyd took him by Frankenstein to build his confidence, but Rex was trembling again, and Lloyd took the team home.

A CAPITAL EVENT

This story came up in the interview: Once in the early 1950s Lloyd had the sled dog team over at the Capitol Building in Sacramento, California. The team had been under the steps, and ran into one of the pillars—hitting it with the side of the sled. A section of the marble pillar tore off above and came down. When it hit the ground it shattered. It just missed hitting and probably killing his friend Al Holden.

A fatal accident could have permanently put the brakes on the White Way sled team....

Rex's Near Fatal Encounter With Future California Governor Jerry Brown

Rex singlehandedly "derailed" a future California Governor *skijoring* up at Truckee. There was a lot of snow on the ground at the time and Lloyd was there with Frank Titus, who was a friend, and Rex, and Lucky, working with several other dogs on the sled.

"Lucky had run out there, turned and come back, showing he didn't want to work under the tough conditions with just anybody." It appears there was a bet or agreement that Lloyd would provide dogs to help in *skijoring*.

"He (Jerry Brown, who was a teenager at the time) came back down there and insisted that I let him have *"that white dog (Rex)"* and I said all right. I figured if I could stay close enough to him with old Lucky it would be OK. But someone came down between us, and next thing I knew I heard a [makes a *shoosh* sound] and it was old Rex going into overdrive gear, and pulling Jerry Brown, who had fallen on the ground on them skis! (AUTHOR'S NOTE: In those days some skis didn't come with quick and effective emergency releases).

"He had the skis behind him, the snow was piled up…them white posts…the steel posts…sticking up, and that sucker (Rex) took him (Jerry Brown) right down that line…for about 4 posts…God almighty, just tore his clothes all off. We took him to the hospital. Old Larry (Dr. Nelson) got him and (Lloyd laughs and rubs his eyes) and finally we had to take him to Reno…and get some help to sew him up.

"When they said they don't know what was the matter with him, well I said, 'I *know* what's the matter with him! (laughs). Yeah, that's him (Jerry Brown).' This was back in the old days, when he was going to high school."

In retrospect, it appears that young Jerry Brown, Jr. couldn't keep up with the "Ferrari" model he had out front of him setting the pace, and continue to stay *upright* on his skis. We will give the future California Governor his due, though, for taking a try at the new winter sport of *skijoring*, where a person is led by a dog, horse, or vehicle on skis over the snow or ice.

Rex Was *Not* Perfect!

Rex had a number of great heroic and admirable qualities about him, but he was *not* without flaws. He wanted to feel that communion with Nature and he needed to work. He had a certain "disconnect" with the crowds, as he didn't feel close to the crowd sometimes at parades and similar events. As Mel Price, former SCA President remarked in an interview, "Rex felt a bond in working close to the earth as befitting his animal nature, and he definitely had the ability to survive in the wild by himself. He was always reported to be fine in the show ring, but he needed to be working to feel fulfilled."

As Lloyd once remarked, *"In a crowd he was nothing."*

In the *Organization for Working Samoyeds The Yapper,* August 1972, Mel wrote:

(I) thought Rex hated crowds. Lloyd said in a crowd he was nothing, (but) a hundred yards out on the trail, and he was tail-up and full of go...(and quoting Lloyd), "He would climb a tree if I said so."

Like all the Van Sickle dogs, he was a trail breaker and trail breaking is hard in this country. The dogs are often in over their shoulders. There was no choice for Rex, as nobody had snowmobiles in this time. Lloyd would break a snowshoe track to show the dogs the direction, and from there on out they did the rest. Rex led Hounds as much as he led Huskies or Sams. None of the Sams from the kennel were equal to him in any respect.

On the mail runs in Idaho and Montana, he was equal to the Targhee Hounds that backed him. He may have been spelled off by a hound named Red that was also a favorite of Lloyd's. In parades and exhibitions, Rex's brother Toby was sometimes used. He was a showman who would trot along, tail up, unlike Rex who sometimes didn't warm up to the crowd as much as Toby.

Lloyd let Rex run loose a lot at his place. When Rex was taken down to Mrs. Mason for a dog show (he was looking pretty good at one point and Mrs. Mason reclaimed him), Rex waited until Agnes went to dinner from the motel and then went through the window to get free. He would be wandering around in front of the hotel when she came back. (AUTHOR'S NOTE: Based upon several references, Rex had a habit of flying through windows and may have done it frequently.)

Per Mel, Lloyd also said, "You can't improve anything by cross-breeding a Sam." She never figured out if this meant you couldn't breed anything better than a Sam, or whether it would be a handicap to the poor pups to have Sam blood in them. Lloyd was always consistently polite to Sam owners no matter what they showed him. (But) on the side, he might say, "Those bench legged feists (small dogs)."

Mel concludes: "We should all be so lucky to have a Leader of his (Rex's) caliber. Despite his initial slightly unusual features, he came within a hair's breadth (of a judge's opinion) of finishing his championship. Nothing would have suited Mrs. Mason better."

When I first came across Mel Fishback's assessments of Rex of losing a race or being skittish in front of crowds, I called Michael Kanyon and asked what he thought. We agreed that I had to keep the material in the story, as otherwise I would not be doing a credible job as historian. The flaws give texture, richness, and layering to the Rex story.

All of our heroes have some flaws if we dig deep enough. Growing up, I remember reading with much interest the biographies of Babe Ruth, Lou Gehrig, and Mel Ott. For me, Clemente, Mazeroski, and Groat "were" the Pittsburgh Pirates, and they had to overcome a long losing tradition before they beat the dreaded Yankees in 1960. Stan Musial was born "down the road" from where I was brought up but he wasn't a Pirate. That probably was his only flaw, but an important one.

Bobby Layne, Buddy Dial, Ernie Stautner, and Jack Butler "were" the Pittsburgh Steelers, and there were a lot of those 4th down and 30 yards-to-go situations when the Steelers were struggling in the late 1950s and early 1960s. Then the Steelers hit it big in the 1970s and everyone in Pittsburgh rallied around the winners... because we all like to be associated with winners.

Modern times have witnessed some of our sports, entertainment, and political heroes and leaders come crashing down from the top, brought about by steroids, substance abuse, or poor lifestyle choices. Babe Ruth had his eating and drinking problems. Stonewall Jackson had his eccentricities, but that didn't detract from his genius on the battlefield. Roberto Clemente told a sportswriter near the end of his playing days that there is no telling how good he could have been if he didn't have to play through pain every day.

The luster of my heroes has not diminished over time, and with regard to Rex, having flaws made him real and believable. Otherwise, we don't have a complete picture of Rex.

PHOTOGRAPH BY DAWN PASINSKI.
COURTESY JIM CHESKAWICH.
WITH APPRECIATION TO WARNER BROS. AND 20TH CENTURY FOX.

CHAPTER 11

WORKING WITH "THE DUKE"

Lloyd took work whenever and however he could find it. With a versatile and well-trained dog sled team, he was creative in putting the dogs to work. He had Targhee Hounds and Malamutes at home, plus a growing family to feed.

1953 WORKING WITH "THE DUKE"

Always on the lookout for work assignments for Rex and the team, Lloyd got the team a job moving props on the set for the *Island in the Sky* movie with John Wayne. Also featured in the film are James Arness, Andy Devine, Lloyd Nolan, and Fess Parker. John Wayne acts against type in the movie and is more down to earth and realistic. It is an unusual yet interesting "Duke" movie.

Initially, obtaining a copy of this film to review and search for Rex was very difficult as the estate of John Wayne had been tied up for over two decades. During that time, *Island in the Sky* could not be shown in movie theaters, on television, or made available in DVD or VCR format. Finally, the estate was settled (after we had worked on Rex for a few years) and the black-and-white print was made available to the general public. Another Wayne movie that was also tied up in the estate dispute was *The High and the Mighty*—which is considered the "granddaddy" of all airplane disaster movies.

Rex doesn't actually appear in *Island in the Sky* and is not listed under screen credits. The film's setting was Quebec-Labrador and John Wayne played the plane pilot who went down with the plane and crew. Rex was hired for "movie-production assistance work," and "guard duty" for John Wayne on location of the filming at Donner Lake, California.

Aljean said in an *SQ* interview that, yes, Rex served as guard dog for John Wayne on the movie set, but she said he was not much of a guard dog.... "He was more of a PUSSYCAT!"

John Wayne was so taken with Rex, that he kept him on location for three additional months and Rex stayed with him in the trailer. It is reasonable to assume that all of the cast members enjoyed Rex's companionship while on the set.

And Lloyd probably told "The Duke" to leave the windows open for Rex at night … or pay up in the morning for broken windows… as Rex was a creature of habit and liked his nightly escapades!

OTHER HOLLYWOOD CONNECTIONS

During the interview with Lloyd in 2004, Lloyd provided pictures of Rin-Tin-Tin and Lassie sitting on a sled being pulled by Rex of White Way. Rin-Tin-Tin was a passenger in Rex's sled down in Riverside, California. Rex was also set up with Lloyd several times in booths next to Roy Rodgers and Dale Evans. Rex never appeared in these particular television programs (that we know of).

But… he knew his way around the Truckee Airfield, Targhee Pass, Donner Lake and the *City of San Francisco,* the Hilltop Lodge and the High Sierras, and he was "The World Record Holder in Weight Pulling." He wasn't taking a back seat to any celluloid created dog!

REX GIVES RIN-TIN-TIN A RIDE!

ROY ROGERS AND DALE EVANS MEET SOME SAMOYEDS.

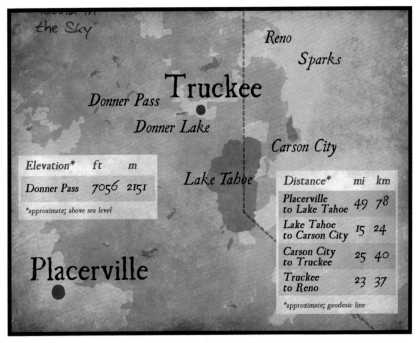

the Sky"

Reno

Sparks

Donner Pass **Truckee**

Donner Lake

Carson City

Elevation*	ft	m
Donner Pass	7056	2151

*approximate; above sea level

Lake Tahoe

Distance*	mi	km
Placerville to Lake Tahoe	49	78
Lake Tahoe to Carson City	15	24
Carson City to Truckee	25	40
Truckee to Reno	23	37

*approximate; geodesic line

Placerville

ILLUSTRATION BY BRAD JOHNSON.

"HAVE (HARNESS), WILL TRAVEL"

After reviewing the tape of the "Alaska" episode several times of the "Have Gun, Will Travel" television series starring Richard Boone as Palladin, Rex clearly appears to be the team Leader of the White Way Team. At one point, Rex pretends to have an injured paw that is bandaged.

The 22-minute segment features dog sled races, a lot of snow, Palladin, and a beautiful team of Samoyeds—led by Rex.

OTHER EXPLOITS AND ADVENTURES

Rex appeared in downtown Truckee, Lake Tahoe, and Tahoe City. He pulled a 400-pound "Queen for a Day" float up a ramp once by sled, had gigs at the Hollywood Bowl and Gilmore Stadium, and was pretty well known in arenas and stadiums throughout California and Nevada. He seemed to like traveling, and all the attention given a Superstar.

Nowadays, the kids would call him a *Rockstar*!

THE MASON SAMOYED TEAM ON HOLLYWOOD BOULEVARD!

LLOYD, REX (TO THE LEFT), AND ANOTHER WHITE WAY KENNEL SAMOYED AT DEL MAR. WE BELIEVE THIS IS THE LAST PICTURE TO BE TAKEN OF REX.

CHAPTER 12

1957:
THE DEL MAR ARENA EXHIBITION
AND...REX'S PASSING

As A Backdrop...

Congress approved the Civil Rights Act of 1957 on April 29th. The U.S. Surgeon General July 12 said studies showed a "direct link" between cigarette smoking and lung cancer. National Guardsmen were called in by Arkansas Governor Orval Faubus, September 4 to bar black students from entering an all-white high school in Little Rock. President Eisenhower signed Civil Rights Act into law September 9, providing for creation of Civil Rights Commission. Jack Kerouac's *On the Road* was published. The Soviet Union launched "Sputnik." On the screen are *12 Angry Men*, *The Ten Commandments*, and *Bridge Over the River Kwai*. Dr. Seuss (Theodore Seuss Geisel) has a popular book out called *The Cat in the Hat*. James Travis (Jim) Reeves records "Four Walls" and Little Richard ("Tutti Frutti"), and Buddy Holly and the Crickets ("That'll Be the Day").

THE DEL MAR ARENA

Lloyd told us in the interview that they were down in Del Mar for Rex's last exhibition. "They have the arena, flag pole, and a big cement (piece) in the middle with a flag on it. Bleachers were all around, they had horse show buggies, and a bandstand.

"That last night I had 11 dogs in the ring and circled the group. I am not bragging, I'm just stating the facts. I have never seen any animal work as good as Rex that night. He must have known that we were all through that night.

"I'd bring him (Rex) around, bring him half way back, straighten him out again...I'd tell him gee a little...look over here, gee...and that sucker, he understood every word I said. I never saw anything like it. I've seen a lot of animals in there but I never saw nothing that beat that.

"Mrs. Mason was crying, all the way out there, just crying, and I thought...*no one couldn't...couldn't do no better*. I never saw anything like he did that night.

"I turned him loose and got up on (a vehicle) and drove him to the mic...and never even stayed with the sled. I run out of stuff to do (with him). I couldn't think of anything that would be difficult...that sucker, he must have known...something...was on. He knew when I was talking to him."

Lloyd said that he "turned the dog team over to Mrs. Mason that night," as he had done "all he could do with them," and he had a wife and family of three kids now to take care of. "I was [located] up in the snow bank and so I...well, that was the last.

I said, *"You can't beat this, Mrs. Mason. They're all yours."*

The average lifespan today for a Samoyed is generally 12–14 years. Some have lived active and fulfilled lives up to age 15 or 16. Others, because of cancer or some other disease, leave us too early. As someone from the distant past used to say, it is good that the dogs don't live a long life like humans who can easily reach 75 or 80. We grieve them terribly when they pass at 12 or so. If they lived to be 80, we would never get over their deaths.

Rex died in August of 1957 at the age of 11.

CHAPTER 13

AFTERMATH

Lloyd said that he believed that Rex died of a broken heart because he lived to work with Lloyd, and that Rex thought Lloyd had abandoned him when he was sent back to Mrs. Mason. Rex stayed on for a few months before passing away.

In the interview, Lloyd said that it was only a few months before Rex died after Lloyd had taken all the dogs back to Mrs. Mason following their last performance at the Del Mar Exhibition. "She said I ought to have Rex, and I told her, 'No, keep your team together. Aljean could do something with them.'

"A while later, I had to go down over to the valley and I stopped in there, and she was in tears. Rex was lying on the floor. She said he hadn't eaten…he wasn't doing nothing…and I sat down there and talked to him…and his eyes opened…and pretty soon his head raised …and I laid him over my lap.

"I had to go someplace, Vallejo or someplace…and I said well, I'll come pick him up on the way home…she said he hadn't eaten for a week.

"When I came back, he was dead."

Lloyd and Agnes were deeply affected by Rex's passing.

However, death is inevitable for all of us and has to be faced. As Mel Fishback offered, "Rex led himself a pretty good life." We should hope all our dogs could live it up like Rex—and still be remembered more than a half-century after their death.

From a conversation Agnes had many years ago with fellow Samoyed owner Kay Ketchum, who is a niece of Lloyd's and who also worked for Agnes when she was a young girl, there is a part of White Way Kennels that Agnes referred to as "sacred ground." Kay told me that this is where Rex's body is most likely buried. She thinks it is in the spot located directly behind the house, behind where a vegetable garden once existed. Agnes would have been able to dig deep enough there, and also she would have been "closer" to Rex from the house and able to walk there. Kay later obtained King Pin, who was a descendant of Rex's.

THE ROAD AND ENTRANCE TO THE OLD WHITE WAY KENNELS.
THE HOUSE IS IN FRONT OF THE FENCE TO THE LEFT.
PHOTOGRAPHS BY JIM WEILAND.
USED BY PERMISSION OF THE OWNER.

Lloyd said that he always felt that Rex was his dog, and likewise Rex felt that he belonged to, and with, Lloyd. Lloyd said at another point in our 2004 interview: "*We kind of had an understanding...you know...you get ...to some of them....*" One of the things Lloyd was most emphatic about was his ownership of Rex. He never owned the AKC papers, but he owned the dog.

Lloyd stated in the interview in 2004 that "After Rex...I made up my mind then...that I'd never get that close to another animal.

"Well...I have to stop now...I'm sorry...*I didn't think I could ever tell that again....*" (Lloyd was in tears, after almost 50 years since Rex's passing.)

In retrospect, even though Rex only lived to be about 11 years of age, this was pretty good for the time when the life expectancy was 8–12. The toll on Rex from high altitude work may have been a factor. Mel Fishback assumes that Rex led himself a good life. "Rex was the gee-haw dog ultimate.

"*Rex was...*" to quote Lloyd, "*a damn fine dog.*"

Lloyd Van Sickle passed away of double pneumonia on December 26, 2006 at age 88.

THE TWO FRIENDS.

HONORING REX

A Memorial To
Rex of White Way

1948 Winner of Children's Race
Leader of Freight Race
Lead on U.S. Mail Team
Leader of Exhibition at the California State Fair

1949 Leader of winning team at the Truckee Races
Led rescue team to plane crash at Truckee, California
The Cedars rescue
Leader of team into Ever Valley snow removal rescue

1950 Hollywood Sportsman's Show Exhibition
Nevada Day Parade, Carson City
March of Dimes Exhibit, San Francisco
Homecoming Parade, University of California
Leader of runner-up team at the Truckee Races

1952 Leader of Winning team at San Mateo Show and leader of
25-dog team.
Removed from bench of Golden Gate Kennel Club Show to
take doctors to snow-bound train in the Sierra Mountains.

1953 Led a team of Targhee Hounds to win the West Yellowstone
Dog Derby
Worked as Leader in team pulling 600-pound loads to
Repair Donner Lake piers in winter emergency
Movie work and guard duty for John Wayne on location
for *Island in the Sky* motion picture

1954 Broke the World Record Weight Pulling Contest with 1,870
pounds

1956 Winner of several events at the Big Bear Valley Sled Races
Won several show points and one major.

1957 Died in August.

RENDERING BY DESTA GARRETT.

FROM ROBERT AND DOLLY WARD, *THE NEW COMPLETE SAMOYED*,
AND FROM THE GERTRUDE ADAMS PAPERS.
THANK YOU TO MARDEE WARD-FANNING.

CHAPTER 14

1961–1962
"REX PLAQUE" AND
LIST OF ACHIEVEMENTS

Agnes was presented with a framed list of her 25 champions by members of the Samoyed Club of America, Pacific Coast Division: "In appreciation for her great devotion to the Samoyed Breed." As Gertrude Adams reported: "In 1962 at Encino, California at the Annual SCA meeting, Charles Burr and Edwin Adams presented a lovely cherry wood and etched bronze, 14″ by 21″ plaque to Mrs. Agnes Mason as a memorial to Rex of White Way. Engraved thereon were the many important events occurring to this famous dog during his lifetime. The plaque was donated by friends and admirers of Rex of White Way, a Samoyed that was a credit to his breed, and performed feats that no other Samoyed has ever done."

OTHER AWARDS AND RECOGNITIONS

Agnes Mason died in 1970 at age 80. She lived in California for 58 years. To honor the memory of Mrs. Mason, the SCA Board voted to initiate an "Agnes Mason Memorial Trophy" to be awarded annually to the Best of Breed winner at the SCA National Specialty.

Aljean Mason was interviewed in the Spring 1984 in the *Samoyed Quarterly*.

Rex has enjoyed a resurgence of national interest over the past decades. In 1978, Rex appeared as the Centerfold in an issue of the *Samoyed Quarterly*. In 2003, a request was sent to the Citizen Advisory Committee on Stamp Selection for a U.S. postage stamp for Rex (see Appendix C). On September 22, 2005, Rex referenced in the U.S. Congressional Record (see Appendix D). Rex and Lloyd were referenced in the *AKC Gazette* in February 2008 in a feature article about Samoyeds. The docu-drama is currently in production about Rex.

REX'S THREE SONS (LEFT TO RIGHT):
BLAZER, TUCKER'S ROGUE, AND BLITZ.
COURTESY CAROL CHITTUM.

CHAPTER 15

THE LEGACY CONTINUES "REX AND HIS FAMILY"

Rex was perhaps the most famous of all of the Mason breedings. He produced two AKC Champions: Ch. Winter Trail Blazer (Dog) owned by Mr. and Mrs. C. N. Burr and Ch. White Way's Juliet O'Snow Ridge (Bitch) owned by W. R. and L. H. Powell. Of Rex's progeny appearing in modern pedigrees, the most influential were (in rank order): Ch. White Way's Juliet O'Snow Ridge, Winter Trail's Rogue, and White Way's Romeo.

Juliet was bred to Ch. Rokandi of Drayalene producing the Morgan's Ch. Darius King, Ch. Patrice, and Rokete of Drayalene. These have all contributed very good Samoyeds.

Rex bred to Charles Burr's Chastuska of Encino CDX produced the Winter Trail litter—their Ch. Blazer, Blitz, Silver Trinket, and Tucker's Rogue. The three males are on the cover of the Bob and Dolly Ward book, *The New Complete Samoyed*. Trinket, when bred to Burr's Ch. Tarkos Kazan of Encino, was the dam of Winter Trail's Kazana who when bred to the Ward's Ch. Starctic Storm helped make Samoyed history by being the mother of Ch. Kazan of Kentwood, bred by Edwards and owned by the Wards.

According to a listing of Mason litters checked by Gertrude Adams, Rex sired 8 litters, which is more than anyone else in the White Way kennel. When you consider that Rex was absent from the kennel most of the time, he was fairly active within the time constraints afforded him, and he did create his own opportunities. Some of the offspring went to Alaska. There were 7 offspring of note and 15 champion grandchildren.

Some of the breedings may have been "unplanned." It was reported that when a bitch was ready for breeding, Rex would get out of his kennel area, climb up to the kennel roof, walk across the roof, and then drop down to service the bitch in season. Agnes's planned breedings involved careful study of the pedigrees. There were other breedings outside the kennel involving Rex. Mr. and Mrs. Charles Burr used Rex several times at stud.

Rex brought stamina, a working attitude, strength, speed, a willingness to please his master, and intelligence to a breeding program. Rex is behind many great Samoyeds.

Jim Osborn, author, statistician, and engineer, conducted a major computer study of Samoyed pedigrees, completed in 1996. The following information on Rex of White Way is taken from the unpublished research report.

"Rex of White Way contributed about 7% of the current gene pool of the modern Samoyed breed in the United States. He is found some 15 to 25 generations back in the pedigrees of today's dogs (2003).

"His name will be found in the pedigree of just about every American bred Samoyed dog, with his name occurring many, many thousands of times. A total of at least 13 of his progeny appear in modern pedigrees, and possibly one or two more that occur only very, very rarely. Those 13 progeny were produced by 7 different dams." They are as follows on the next page:

OFFSPRING	DAM
Alpine-Glo (b)	Honcha of White Frost
Silver Kolya (b)	White Way Starctic Jill
White Way Starctic Jill (b)	Trooperine of White Way
White Way Yermak (d)	Starchak's Warnistura
Ch. White Way's Julliet O'Snow Ridge (b)	White Way Sisero's Beaux
White Way's Romeo (d)	White Way Starctic Jill
White Way's Snow Boots (d)	Trooperine of White Way
White Way's Snow Sheen (b)	Trooperine of White Way
White Way's Solano (b)	Czarina of White Way
White Way's Sonoma (b)	Czarina of White Way
Ch. Winter Trail Blazer (d)	Chastuska of Encino
Winter Trail's Rogue (d)	Chastuska of Encino
Winter Trail's Silver Trinket (b)	Chastuska of Encino

REX'S SPIRIT AND BLOODLINE LIVES IN NEARLY EVERY SAMOYED
ALIVE TODAY IN THE UNITED STATES.
COURTESY JIM OSBORN.

Jim Osborn's research identified foundation animals and their contribution to the modern gene pool. His analysis was based on dogs born from the 1920s to the early 1970s. Therefore, almost all of the important dogs that show up in the study were born before 1950. A sample of today's dogs would yield additional animals born at later dates, Ono and Riley are among them. The rankings are based on relative contribution to the gene pool, regardless of titles, show records, etc.

DESCENDANTS OF REX, CH. HOOF 'N PAW'S SNOSHU
KNIGHT (THEO) AND SNOSHU'S WHITE ROSE HOOF 'N PAW (SHAYLA),
WORKING SAMOYEDS "AT PLAY"
PULLING A SCOOTER WITH CATHY CUSACK.
PHOTOGRAPH BY TAMARA SOMERVILLE.
COURTESY TAMARA SOMERVILLE.

REX'S DAUGHTER WINTER TRAIL'S SILVER TRINKET.
COURTESY CAROL CHITTUM.

MR. AND MRS. CHARLES BURR SENT OUT A CHRISTMAS AND NEW YEAR'S GREETING
THAT HIGHLIGHTS REX (TO THE LEFT), AND HIS THREE SONS (TO THE RIGHT).
AS THEY SAID, "WE FEEL THERE COULD BE NO BETTER TIME THAN
TO PRESENT OUR TRIBUTE TO A GREAT SAMOYED, REX OF WHITE WAY."
COURTESY CAROL CHITTUM.

DELI, A DESCENDANT OF REX'S, RESTING IN A KIRKLAND PET BED.
PHOTO COURTESY OF COSTCO WHOLESALE CORPORATION
AND RYANN GRADY.
USED WITH PERMISSION.

POSTSCRIPT

As I come to the end of my Rex story, I am sitting at my desk, with Riley close by, thumbing through photographs and newspapers and magazines describing Rex's life...and those who loved him.

Agnes Mason and Lloyd Van Sickle were high achievers, maybe overachievers in many areas. The trio of Agnes, Lloyd, and Rex was pretty hard to beat!

Kay Ketchum said that the pairing up of Lloyd and Rex was like two "ancient warriors" reunited in modern times for new battles and escapades.

Aljean Mason Larson and Alta Van Sickle were super-partners of Agnes and Lloyd respectively, who sometimes had to take the lead themselves.

At about a year old, Rex was the lead dog on the U.S. mail team. That is quite an achievement by itself. At the age of three, Rex was written up as *"The Blizzard King"* and the top do-it-all sled dog for Lloyd! Rex was fast (able to keep up with Targhee Hounds who "couldn't slack him") and set a world record in weight pulling as the strongest dog in the world pound-for-pound.

He was dependable enough to be the lead dog or one of the lead dogs on many critical rescues.

Rex is very important to Samoyed breeding programs although he never became a champion. Perhaps the Samoyed height standard was raised because of Rex, perhaps not. Only Mrs. Mason, who was head of the committee to work on changing the standard, knew for sure. What we can be sure of is that, once it was raised, Rex exemplified through his work successes the reasons for keeping the standard at the new height.

He liked to go through windows and hated being inactive. Rex was much like Lloyd, who also couldn't sit still and remain idle for too long. Rex was clever, highly intelligent, and Agnes did treat him like a human being, from several reports. Rex knew he was good, wanted to please, was wise and very calm, had an aura about him, and some even say he had a certain swagger when he wanted to show off.

With male judges, Rex was all business, knowing that he had to produce. No games or clowning. Around female judges, Rex acted like "an imp." Even though he wasn't trained to "give his paw," he was smart enough to "beg" in the ring for a show win, if he thought it would help. (He could have spent his off time watching Lassie on television, who had that act down cold!) As Alice Lombardi remarked in her interview about Rex, "You don't get a dog who you have to go out and prove is a great specimen of the breed." Rex was a great dog, and everyone in Samoyed circles at the time knew it, and they talked about him in that context, even to the point of embellishment.

As Lloyd told us, Agnes was initially embarrassed about Rex. He was oversized—with "those four long, gangly legs that looked like they came out of one socket." Later, through sheer perseverance and drive, Rex not only excelled as the Leader of numerous sled dog rescues, including the "Modern-Day Donner Party" Rescue of the *City of San Francisco* passenger train when he was six years old, but he also became the "new standard" for Samoyeds in the dog show world—the height standard for male Samoyeds was actually raised from 22 inches to 23½ inches. And Rex left us his exciting and inspiring story!

Rex's story parallels a similar storyline found in the lives in such heroes as Babe Ruth, Roberto Clemente, Abraham Lincoln, Stonewall Jackson, and many, many others. Tremendous obstacles had to be overcome in each of these cases to reach the highest tier. It helps us know that others have been counted "out," risen from the ashes, dusted themselves off, and tried again and again. The Rex story reminds us that we can pull ourselves up and succeed.

Rex was a fine ambassador for the breed, and epitomized that special bond between humans and dogs. He was the "real thing" whose strength and stamina placed him above his peers. Rex was more than just a Samoyed breed of dog with a memorable or catchy name. The Samoyed is a working breed, and Rex became the model of working excellence for the breed. In the hands of master trainer, Lloyd Van Sickle, Rex reached very high levels of sustained performance in many areas. Rex of White Way's legacy was to demonstrate how a well-trained and willing Samoyed could perform in many venues.

And Agnes got her wish…which was to prove that show dogs could be *working dogs*.

In a way, Rex wrote his own story and my job was to be faithful to the marks he left and then to report on his life.

This was a great dog.

COURTESY MIKE BLIDE, COTTONWOOD OWNER/MANAGER.

A HILLTOP *"SIGHTING"* ...

AUGUST 2008 "WHITE DOG" GHOST STORIES
AT HILLTOP LODGE IN TRUCKEE, CALIFORNIA

Based on reports from the Hilltop Lodge (now Cottonwood) in Truckee, California, there are stories of recent appearances over the last few years of "a white dog and a white-haired man" who appear at night, then move through walls, and disappear. We feel as if Rex's spirit is still with us in bringing his story to life, but we need further evidence to prove that the ghost of Rex is still at the Hilltop.

Celinda and I visited Truckee several times once we started researching the Rex story. On our first visit, we had a waitress who told us the story of how the staff was working late one night after closing when someone saw "a white dog" and "an elderly man" passing through the walls back by the restroom. They dropped the trays with the tip money they had collected and ran outside!

The same waitress told us that the day before we arrived at the Hilltop, a hole had mysteriously appeared in the wall of one of the restrooms. The staff had tried to cover up the hole with a picture, but the picture couldn't be straightened and always hung at a tilt. The waitress concluded that the spirit or spirits knew we were coming to visit Rex's old "home" in Truckee. Periodically, unusual incidents occur at the Hilltop. Only children and the elderly can see the ghosts now, as the stories were told to us.

The dinner menu has a picture of a sled on it, and the walls are decorated with pictures from the past of snow festivals, Winter Carnivals, ski runs, ice houses, and snow scenes. The Hilltop can claim it was the site of the nation's first mechanized ski lift. From the 1920s until possibly into the 1980s, the Hilltop served as the meeting place for the "Sierra Dog Derby Association," among other clubs devoted to winter sports.

Lloyd's ashes are in an urn—capped by several Samoyeds—resting comfortably on the mantlepiece at son Steve's place.

At the Hilltop, the fireplace and restaurant décor are definitely from another long-ago era. Walking through the main entrance, one can be instantly transported back to the magical time when Lloyd and Rex used this place as "Command Central"...and a launching-off point for rescuing cracked up planes at Truckee Airfield, delivering medical services to the socked-in *City of San Francisco* up at the Donner Pass, or for lesser-known Rex rescues such as Ever Valley and Cedars, among others.

If Rex's ghost is still patrolling The Hilltop Lodge in Truckee, California, it is only because he is waiting for another chance to be hooked up and placed as the Leader to go chase down one of Lloyd's new adventures!

After all, The Hilltop Lodge was the hangout for many years for Rex and his pal Lloyd.

Courtesy Mike Blide, Cottonwood Owner/Manager.

FOREVER FRIENDS.

Jim Cheskawich and Riley.
Photograph by Minette Siegel.

ABOUT
THE
AUTHOR

Jim Cheskawich was born and raised in western Pennsylvania. He received his B.S. in Business Management and his MBA from Penn State. In between, he served with the 101st Airborne Division in the U.S. Army in Vietnam. After nearly 28 years with the Federal government in Washington, DC, he retired in 2002 as the Human Resources Director for Mine Safety and Health Administration under the U.S. Department of Labor.

Jim currently manages Woodland Kennels in Woodland, WA and has worked as a substitute teacher for nearly ten years, working with pre-school students up to the 12th grade.

He served as Samoyed Club of America (SCA) president for three years and lost track of how many years he served as SCA treasurer. He has been local club (Willamette Valley Samoyed Fanciers) president for 6–7 years, and is currently local club treasurer. With the exception of an 8-month period, he has served as the SCA Education and Research Foundation treasurer since its formation in 1998.

BIBLIOGRAPHY, REFERENCES, AND SOURCES

Ralph Waldo Emerson, Essays and Lectures, Literary Classics of the United States, Inc. New York, N.Y. 1983, Penguin Group (USA) Inc. The American Scholar Oration delivered before the Phi Beta Kappa Society at Cambridge, Massachusetts, August 31, 1837. Emerson quote from pages 56 and 57 of the book determined by the Emerson book publisher to be in the public domain: Page ix.

Susan J. Crockford, Ph.D., University of Victoria, BC, Canada, from correspondence notes: Pages 8, 9, 10, 11.

Helen Corlew Newman, Petersburg, ND: Pages 61, 62, 63, and 64 for Dog Sled Terms. From correspondence notes: Pages 55, 56, 58, 60, 66, 68.

Mark McLaughlin, Weather Historian/Author/Professional Speaker. Tahoe Nuggets: Pages 103, 104, 105, 106, 107, 108, 109, 110, 111, 112, 113, 114, 115, 116, 117. Internet site: www.thestormking.com; Blog: www.tahoenuggets.com.

Western Kennel World magazine (*WKW*) 1938–1958 issues. Vera Lawrence, Samoyed Column Editor, San Francisco, California (no longer in publication): Pages 24, 76, 77, 78, 80, 84, 85, 87, 88, 97, 99, 100, 101, 120, 122, 128, 129.

The Samoyed Quarterly, Various Issues 1977–2011, Hoflin Publishing Company, Arvada, Colorado: Pages 18, 28, 29, 30, 31, 32, 33, 34, 35, 36, 37, 38, 41, 103, 105, 106, 132, 133, 135, 136, 139.

The New Complete Samoyed by Robert H. and Dolly Ward, 1986, Howell Book House, New York, New York: Pages xiii, xxiv, 3, 4, 12, 13, 14, 15, 17, 18, 20, 22, 37, 56, 58, 65, 66, 67, 68, 82, 83, 84, 85, 88, 93, 119, 124, 125, 150, 153, 154.

Samoyed Club of America Bulletins 1945–2011, Samoyed Club of America. Various Editors-Peggy Borcherding, Jill Smoot, Cheryl West, Celinda Cheskawich, Lisa Oakman, Modern Litho, Jefferson City, Missouri: Pages 75, 77, 78, 79, 80, 81,116, 119, 120.

Rhythms of Life, Thyroid Hormone and the Origin of Species, Susan J. Crockford, Ph.D., 2006, Trafford Publishing, Victoria, BC, Canada: Page 10.

The World Almanac and Book of Facts 2012, World Almanac Books, Sarah Janssen, Senior Editor, New York, New York: Pages 71, 78, 79, 103, 119, 125, 128, 145.

American Decades, 1940–1949 and 1950–1959, A Manley, Inc. Book, Brucoli and Layman, 1994 and 1995, By Gale Research, Inc. 835 Penobscot Building, Detroit, MI 48226: Pages 76, 78, 79, 101, 103, 119, 125, 128, 145.

Internet site for historical yearly events: 1946–1957. http://www.thepeople history.com.

The Savvy Samoyed, Pat Hill Goodrich, 2001, Doral Publishing, Sun City, Arizona: Pages 19, 23, 31, 35, 39.

American Kennel Club (AKC) Gazette, February 2008, Sheila Goffe article on Samoyeds and Rex of White Way: Pages 105, 107.

Mush, A Beginner's Manual of Sled Dog Training, April 1997, Edited by Bella Levorsen, Sierra Nevada Dog Driver's Inc.: Page 57.

Training Lead Dogs, Lee and Mel Fishback, Tun-Dra, Nunica, Michigan, 1979: Pages 59, 60, 65, 66, 67.

Snowbound Streamliner, Rescuing the 1952 City of San Francisco, Robert J. Church, 2004, Signature Press, Wilton, California: Page 110.

Interview Notes with Lloyd and Steve Van Sickle, Klamath Falls, Oregon, 2004: Pages 1, 41, 42, 43, 44, 46, 50, 51, 56, 57, 69, 72, 73, 74, 75, 77, 78, 81, 88, 91, 107, 108, 109, 111, 119, 122, 123, 124, 125, 126, 131, 132, 133, 134, 135, 136, 137, 140, 142, 145, 146, 147, 149, 160, 163.

Interview/E-mail/Telephone Conversation Notes with Kay Ketchum, Alta Van Sickle, Sara Van Sickle Dexter, Alice Lombardi, Doris McLaughlin, Wilna Coulter, Leona Powell Pedersen, Mardee Ward-Fanning, Mel Price, Pat deBack, Sandie Flettner 2004–2012: Pages 1, 72, 73, 74, 106,111,126, 132, 147.

Original Pages of Gertrude Adams' Private Collection (1910–1970) articles, memorabilia, and notes: Pages 22, 29, 37, 38, 70, 73, 100, 101, 120, 121, 150, 151, 153, 154.

Jim Osborn Statistical Reports on Samoyed Foundation Dogs, 2004–5, Northridge, California: Pages 16, 21, 154, 155.

American Kennel Club Online Breeder Classifieds-Printable Puppy Buying Sheet, Educational Information, http://www.akc.org/breeds/puppy, 1/30/2012: Page 11.

Dog Fancy, March 2012, "Out of the Wild" by Cheryl Langlois: Page 9.

Discovery News, Prehistoric Dog Domestication Derailed by Ice Age, Jennifer Viegas, July 28, 2011: Page 8 http://news.discovery.com/animals/dog-domestication-prehistoric-ice-age.

National Geographic Daily News, Ancient Dog Skull Shows Early Pet Domestication, Christine Dell'Amore, 8/20/2011, http://news.nationalgeographic.com/news/2011/08/110819-dogs-wolves-russia-domestication.

PLOS One: A 33,000-Year-Old Incipient Dog from the Altai Mountains of Siberia: Evidence of the Earliest Domestication Disrupted by the Last Glacial Maximum, Research Article, Co-Authored: Nikolai D. Ovodov, Susan J. Crockford, Yaroslav V. Kuzmin, Thomas F. G. Higham, Gregory W. L. Hodgins, Johannes van der Plicht: Page 8.

Science-AAAS, American Association for the Advancement of Science, The Chinese Wolf, Ancestor of New World Dogs, Stanley J. Olsen and John W. Olsen, August 5, 1977, http://www.jstor.org/stable/1745041.

Dogs Through Time: An Archaeological Perspective, Proceedings of the 1st ICAZ Symposium on the History of the Domestic Dog, Edited by Susan Janet Crockford, Ph.D., August 23–29, 1998, Victoria, B.C., Canada: Page 7, 8.

Journal of Archaeological Science, Fossil Dogs and Wolves from Palaeothic Sites in Belgium, the Ukraine and Russia: Osteometry, Ancient DNA and Stable Isotopes, 2009, Mietje Germonpre, Mikhail V. Sablin, Rhiannon E. Stevens, Robert E. M. Hedges, Michael Hofreiter, Mathias Stiller, Viviane R. Despres.

d'Keta Samoyeds Website, History of the Breed, http://dketasamoyeds.com.

Organization for the Working Samoyed Newsletter, The Yapper, August 1972, Judy Schirber Publisher, Boonville, New York: Pages 73, 94, 111, 136.

Team and Trail Magazine, Publisher, Bicknell, Out of Print, Articles by Mel Fishback Riley, 1970–1979.

The Complete Pedigree Book of American Champion Samoyeds, 1907–1971, Volumes One and Two, Trustees of the Goodrich Fund, Straus Printing Company, Madison, Wisconsin, October 1975, Bob and Wanda Krauss: Page 20, 22, 23.

Agnes Mason Letter of Appreciation to Members of the Samoyed Club of America, August 2, 1952: Pages 18, 30, 30, 31, 50, 121.

Sprague River, Oregon Newspaper, April 15, 2004: Pages 41, 42.

Northern Dog News (NDN), December 1974, Mel Fishback article (now defunct publication): Pages 46, 47, 48, 49, 71, 72, 73.

Rex of White Way Pedigree, Bob Hupp Pedigree Research Work: Appendix F, Pages 203, 204.

Sacramento Bee Newspaper, Sacramento, CA, Feb. 1, 1949: Pages 82 and 83.

Oakland Tribune Newspaper, Oakland, CA, January 17, 1952: Page 114.

Farthest North, Dr. Fridjof Nansen, 1897, Harper and Brothers Publishers, New York and London.

In Nacht Und Eis, Fr. Nansen, Leipzig, 1898, F. A. Brockhaus.

Samoyeds, W. Lavallin Puxley, 1947, Lund Humphries, London, England.

The Complete Dog Book of the American Kennel Club, 19th Edition Revised, 1998, Howell Book House, Foster City, California: Page 13.

Samoyed Champion Pedigrees, U.S.A., 1907–1971, Lila Weir, Roberta Hoernig, Marj Van Ornum, 1977, The Bastion Press, Olympia, Washington.

How to Raise and Train a Samoyed, Vera Kroman, 1964, T. F. H. Publications, Neptune City, New Jersey.

Samoyeds, Joyce Reynaud, 1988, T. F. H. Publications, Neptune City, New Jersey.

Your Samoyed, Jan Kauzlarich, 1977, Denlinger's, Fairfax, Virginia.

Susan Amundson, Hastings, Minnesota, "A Samoyed Tribute," 1999: Page xiv.

The Samoyed, The Samoyed Association, 1995, Geoff Grounds, Rivers Media Services Limited, Piccadilly, London, Great Britain.

All About the Samoyed, Beryl and Geoff Grounds, 1998, Kingdom Books, England.

The Complete Samoyed, Robert H. and Dolly Ward, 1972, Howell Book House, New York, New York.

The New Samoyed, Robert H. and Dolly Ward and Mardee Ward-Fanning, 1998, Howell Book House, New York, New York.

The Dog Lovers' Book, Edwin Noble, Undated (circa 1904), Dana, Estes and Co., Boston, Massachusetts.

Brazilian Pet Magazine, No 308 Caes and Cia, Fabio Bense Publisher, 2004–5 co-written article on Samoyeds by Jim and Celinda Cheskawich.

This Is the Samoyed, Joan Brearley, 1975, T. F. H. Publications, Neptune City, NJ.

Hutchinson on Samoyeds, Walter Hutchinson, Reprinted 1976, Donald R. Hofflin, Arvada, Colorado.

Samoyed Club of America Historical Archives Materials maintained by Steve Loper, Yelm, Washington.

Samoyed Pedigrees, Volumes 1–3, 1901–1990, Samoyed Association of Great Britain and printed by Warwick Savage Ltd., Burslem, Stoke-on-Trent, 1960, 1974, 1990.

American Kennel Club website www.AKC.org: Page 36.

Samoyed Club of America/AKC Flyer: Welcome to the Wonderful World of Samoyeds, 2010: Pages 199–202.

Through a Dog's Eyes, Jennifer Arnold, 2011, Spiegel and Grau, New York.

University of San Francisco Website http://www.usfca.edu/templates/ocm_media_relations: Page 79.

General Reference Books on Sledding:

1. *Alone Across the Arctic* by Pam Flowers, Graphic Arts Center Publishing Company.

2. *The Joy of Running Sled Dogs* by Noil K. Flanders.

3. *Dog Driver: A Guide for the Serious Musher* by Miki and Julie Collins.

PHOTOGRAPHY, ILLUSTRATIONS, AND ARTWORK CREDITS FOR REX BOOK

PAGE NO.	CITATION	SOURCE/PERMISSION
Front Cover	Rex and Lloyd	Lloyd and Steve Van Sickle
Front Cover	Rex Mushing	Lloyd and Steve Van Sickle
Back Cover	Dog Sled	Kay Ketchum, Lloyd and Alta Van Sickle
Author Photo	Jim Cheskawich and Riley	Minette Siegel
iv	Rex Jumping on Lloyd	Lloyd and Steve Van Sickle
vi	Rex and Aljean Mason	Lloyd and Steve Van Sickle
x	Dog Sled Team	Nan Holt Artwork, with permission
xiv	Samoyed Puppy	English Artwork from Crufts Photo by Noel Johnson Courtesy Jim Cheskawich
xviii	Alta and Rex	Lloyd and Steve Van Sickle
xx	Joanne Carolan Artwork	Jim Cheskawich photo Courtesy Jim and Celinda Cheskawich
xxii	Rex Sled Team	Lloyd and Steve Van Sickle
xxiii	*Western Kennel World* and other magazines	Jim Cheskawich photo Courtesy Jim and Celinda Cheskawich
xxiii	BISS Seattle	Steven Ross Photo, with permission
xxvi	Rex after Weight Pull, the Keyboard Picture	Mardee Ward-Fanning, with permission Courtesy Jim Cheskawich
xxvii	Lloyd and Steve	Michael Kanyon
xxviii	Ono and Riley	Photo by Ken O'Brien Courtesy Heather Kelly
xxix	Rex and Lloyd	Courtesy Gail Spieker
xxx	Rex Leading Team	Lloyd and Steve Van Sickle
Page 5	Rex in Snow in Idaho	Courtesy Kay Ketchum
Page 6	"On the Move"	Original black-and-white sketch by Pam Landers. Photo by Norma Pinkert. Courtesy Pam Landers

Page 11	Samoyed on Ski	Truckee Donner Historical Society Truckee Chamber of Commerce, and thank you to Frank Rossback
Page 12	Greenland Scenery Porcelain Plate	Courtesy Jim Cheskawich Photo by Noel Johnson
Page 14	Russian Ceramic	Courtesy Jim and Celinda Cheskawich Photo by Noel Johnson
Page 15	Aljean Mason and Rex's Sire	*Western Kennel World* magazine Courtesy Jim and Celinda Cheskawich
Page 17	Ch. Ice Crystal of the Arctic – A Pastel by Faith Harris Child	Courtesy Jim Cheskawich Photo by Noel Johnson
Page 19	Aljean Mason and Czar Nicholas	*Samoyed Quarterly,* Spring 1984
Page 20	Agnes Mason and Samoyeds	Jim Osborn/North Cal Sam Club
Page 20	Ch. Herdsman's Faith	*Pedigree Book of American Champion Samoyeds* Courtesy Bob and Wanda Krauss
Page 23	Col. Soldier Frosty of Rimini	Courtesy Pat deBack and Pat Hill Goodrich
Page 26	Stained Glass Lamp	Sal Lawrence, MD, Glass Works Artist Photo by Noel Johnson Courtesy Jim Cheskawich
Page 27	Russian Wood Carving	Courtesy Jim Cheskawich Photo by Noel Johnson
Page 27	Greg and Julia Ketchum and King Pin	Courtesy Kay Ketchum
Page 28	Aljean Mason and Rex	*Samoyed Quarterly,* Spring 1984
Page 31	Dogs in Defense	Courtesy Sandie Flettner and Pat Hill Goodrich, *The Savvy Samoyed,* with permission
Page 32	Rex at Donner Summit	Lloyd and Steve Van Sickle
Page 34	White Way Sams	Jim Osborn
Page 34	Christmas Greetings	*Western Kennel World*
Page 35	A "White" Christmas	*Western Kennel World*
Page 36	Hotel Senator Gathering	*Western Kennel World*
Page 38	California State Fair	Courtesy Pat deBack and Pat Hill Goodrich *The Savvy Samoyed,* with permission
Page 39	Three Team Photos	Courtesy Kay Ketchum

Page 40	Lloyd and Rex	Lloyd and Steve Van Sickle
Page 43	Rex and Team at Hilltop Lodge	Courtesy Carol Chittum
Page 43	Old Hilltop Lodge	Courtesy Mark McLaughlin
Page 44	Rex after Winning Speed Race	Lloyd and Steve Van Sickle
Page 45	Alta and Steve Van Sickle	Photo by Sara Van Sickle Dexter Courtesy Sara Van Sickle Dexter
Page 49	Lloyd at Interview	Michael Kanyon
Page 51	Lloyd and Baby Rex	Courtesy Kay Ketchum
Page 52	Lloyd & Rex in Idaho	Lloyd and Steve Van Sickle
Page 53	Samoyed Ceramic Flask	Photo by Noel Johnson Courtesy Jim Cheskawich
Page 54	Truckee Sled Dog Races Poster (circa 1925)	Producer Harold McCoy Artist: Ken Eberts
Page 59	9 Way Fan Hitch Greenland Plate	Courtesy Jim Cheskawich Photo by Noel Johnson
Page 61,63,64	Dog Sled Diagram and Dog Sled Terms	Courtesy Helen Corlew Newman
Page 62	Nan Holt Dog Sled Line-up	Original illustration by Nan Holt Courtesy Nan Holt
Page 70	Sandy Van Sickle with Rex	Courtesy Sara Van Sickle
Page 74	Rex Saving the Day!	Lloyd and Steve Van Sickle
Page 82,83	Dog Teams Rescue Four February 1, 1949.	Permission from *Sacramento Bee* Copyright McClatchey News Services, 1949 Thank you to Tami Berget
Page 86	Oski-Berkeley Bear with Friend	Courtesy of The Bancroft Library University of California, Berkeley Thank you to Lorna Kirwan Used by permission
Page 89	Russian Ceramic	Courtesy Jim Cheskawich Photo by Noel Johnson
Page 90	Rex and Mail Team	Courtesy Carol Chittum
Page 92	Mail Run Route Map	Illustration by Brad Johnson
Page 94	Rex and Lloyd on Mail Run	Lloyd and Steve Van Sickle
Page 96	Rex on Double-Duty	Courtesy Kay Ketchum

Page 98	Rex, Team, and Lloyd	Lloyd and Steve Van Sickle
Page 100/101	Lloyd Letter	*Western Kennel World*, and Gertrude Adams Papers
Page 102	Rescue at Yuba Gap	Original art by Nan Holt. Best in Art Show, SCA 2012 National Courtesy Nan Holt Photograph by Neil Koppes, Mesa, AZ
Page 104	Landscape of Blizzard	Nevada Historical Society Thank you to Lee Brumbaugh
Page 105	Train Trapped on Mountainside	Nevada Historical Society Thank you to Lee Brumbaugh
Page 106	Aerial View	Nevada Historical Society Thank you to Lee Brumbaugh
Page 107	Yuba Gap Area Map	Illustration by Brad Johnson
Page 109	Train in Snow	Nevada Historical Society Thank you to Lee Brumbaugh
Page 113	Ravine	Nevada Historical Society. Thank you to Lee Brumbaugh
Page 114	Drama in the Sierra	Courtesy and Copyrighted, *Oakland Tribune,* Jan 17, 1952, with permission Photographer: Lonnie Wilson Thank you to Veronica Martinez
Page 117	Snow Blower	Photo by Robert Gerdel. Courtesy Mark McLaughlin/Gerdel Collection
Page 118	Rex at Long Beach Show	Lloyd and Steve Van Sickle
Page 122	Sandie Flettner and Agnes Mason	Courtesy Sandie Flettner
Page 123	Rex and Lloyd at Yellowstone	Lloyd and Steve Van Sickle
Page 124	Wood Carving	Artwork by Karen Sickle Trophy from Karen Sickle in honor of Rebel Photo Noel Johnson Courtesy Jim Cheskawich
Page 126	Agnes Mason Card Weight Pulling Win	Courtesy Carol Chittum
Page 127	Samoyed Tribute Medal	Photo by Noel Johnson Courtesy Jim and Celinda Cheskawich
Page 129	March of Dimes	Lloyd and Steve Van Sickle
Page 130	Rex Leaping	Lloyd and Steve Van Sickle

Page 138	John Wayne Poster	Photo by Dawn Pasinski Warner Bros. and 20th Century Fox, with appreciation
Page 140	Rex and Rin-Tin-Tin	Lloyd and Steve Van Sickle
Page 141	Roy Rogers and Dale Evans and Sams	Lloyd and Steve Van Sickle
Page 142	Donner Lake Map	Illustration by Brad Johnson
Page 143	Mason Team on Hollywood Blvd.	Lloyd and Steve Van Sickle
Page 144	Lloyd, Rex, Sams at Del Mar	Lloyd and Steve Van Sickle
Page 148	Road and Entrance to White Way Kennels	Photos by Jim Weiland Used by permission of owner
Page 149	The Two Friends	Lloyd and Steve Van Sickle
Page 150	"Rex Plaque" and List of Achievements	Rendered by Desta Garrett, from Robert and Dolly Ward, *The New Complete Samoyed,* and Gertrude Adams Papers Thank you to Mardee Ward-Fanning
Page 152	Rex's Three Sons	Courtesy Carol Chittum
Page 156	Cathy Cusack and Rex Descendants, Theo and Shayla	Photo by Tamara Somerville Courtesy Tamara Somerville
Page 157	Rex's Daughter	Courtesy Carol Chittum
Page 157	Burr's Season Greetings	Courtesy Carol Chittum
Page 158	Deli and Kirkland Pillow	Costco Wholesale Corporation and Ryann Grady Thank you to PJ (Peggy-Jo) Faria Used with permission
Page 161	Rex after Weight Pull World Record	Mardee Ward-Fanning, with permission Courtesy Jim Cheskawich
Page 162	Cottonwood Bar and Restaurant	Courtesy Mike Blide, Owner/Mgr.
Page 164	Cottonwood Bar and Restaurant	Courtesy Mike Blide, Owner/Mgr.
Page 165	Forever Friends	Lloyd and Steve Van Sickle
Page 166	Jim and Riley	Photo by Minette Siegel Photo taken at The Presidio, San Francisco, CA

Page 179	Riley at the National	Photo by Minette Siegel Photo taken at The Presidio, San Francisco, CA
Page 183	Heather Kelly and Riley	Courtesy Alan Stevenson and Heather Kelly
Page 184	Riley (age 11) Sheep Herding at "Brigand's Hideout"	Courtesy and Photo Jim Cheskawich
Page 188	Alan Stevenson and BISS Ono at National Show	Photo by Ken O'Brien, with permission Courtesy Alan Stevenson
Page 203	Rex leading team at San Mateo	Courtesy Jim Osborn

APPENDIX A

RILEY WITH HIS WINNING RIBBON. PHOTOGRAPH BY MINETTE SIEGEL.

RILEY AT THE NATIONAL

*How to Win a Best in Show at the National
Samoyed Specialty (2011) as an Old Veteran....*

And Living the Life of Riley

"Multi-BISS Ch. d'Keta Strikes Gold, HCT-s"

Riley came out of his retirement as he approached age 10 in January of 2011, when we decided to show him at just the West Coast Samoyed Specialties to "see what he could do." Most Samoyeds are retired by age 5 or 6; some do go on longer in the show ring. Riley is out of the superstar "Ono" (BISS Ch. Oakbrook's Strike It Rich) and Group Placing Cricket (Ch. Sanorka's Trip Into Tamara).

Riley is owned by Jim and Celinda Cheskawich and was bred by Celinda Cheskawich, Janice Hovelmann, and Christie Smith. He had received a Best of Opposite Sex award at the Washington State Samoyed

Specialty at Enumclaw, WA in August 2010 giving an indication that he could …"still be a contender."

We had no idea of what was to come!

His sire, Ono, had won the SCA National in 2000 and had died tragically at age 4 in 2001 when placed in the wrong part of the plane traveling back to California from the first AKC Eukanuba Classic in Orlando, Florida. Ono was considered by many familiar with Samoyeds as "THE DOG" of a generation.

Looking back now on Riley's National win, he seemed to have a destiny to fulfill and it didn't matter how long it was going to take him. We just had to be patient and later we learned to kick back, relax and enjoy the ride! He did get better with age as some judges have said! Riley didn't go to many Nationals due to travel time or Celinda or Christie judging them, so when the time came, he made the most of his opportunity and picked his last show for his best performance!

Previous to 2011, Riley was only shown at the two local Samoyed Specialties each year for several years. As a young pup living with the Stevensons in California, Riley finished his championship fairly easily and took a few Best of Breed wins with Alan at the end of the lead. Heather and Riley went Best Puppy at the SCA National in Denver in 2001 out of about 100 Sams. He knows his way around the ring but wasn't in to showing the first few years and really looked like a puppy until he turned age 8 or 9 years old. He always could move out but was a slow maturing male.

Celinda and Christie Smith used to say if you can find a Sam that moves better than Riley, pull that dog or bitch aside. When Riley was a ten-week-old puppy headed out west from Virginia to Christie in Oregon, Jim just thought he had long legs and would never be anything special. Christie wrote in a letter to Celinda around 2002 that "…This boy is our next Best in Show."

Riley only had one Conformation training class in the last seven to eight years, as he was almost flawless each time in the ring. Jim once lost the lead from his hand at the Willamette Valley Samoyed Fanciers Specialty show in 2010, but Riley continued around the ring without breaking stride as if nothing had happened and then Jim caught up to him. Riley got Best Veteran at the Show.

Jim showed him at a few shows early on in 2003 and 2004 and picked up some Breed wins including the January 2004 Rose City Classic when Riley thereafter ended up on Animal Planet reruns of that show for almost 3 years!

Riley was retired sometime later. He is a happy boy, always wanting to travel, and became an easy keeper, unlike the first couple of years when he tore up mattresses, ripped out walls, barked his head off, and was the "straw that stirred the kennel" with his antics. He was destructive, willful, and too smart for his own good growing up the first 3 years.

The following is Riley's record for his last 8 shows:

August 2010	Wash State Spec	BestOppositeSex/BestVet
Jan 2011	LA Sam Spec	Best Male Vet
March 2011	Ariz Sam Spec	AOM and Best Vet
May 2011	Barbary Coast Spec	Best Vet
June 2011	Nor Cal Spec	Best in Show at a Spec (BISS)
June 2011	Nor Cal Spec	Best Opp Sex at a Spec
June 2011	Willamette Spec (OR)	Best Vet
August 2011	Wash State Spec	Best Vet
Oct 16, 2011	SCA National	Best in Show, Best Vet (BISS)

After his National win in 2011, Riley is now retired and finished 2011 as the #8 Samoyed under one system for *Canine Chronicle*. For the last 9 shows, he won: Two Best in Shows at a Specialty, including the National where there were 316 Samoyeds entered, 2 Best of Opposite Sex awards at Specialties, an Award of Merit, and he was always the Best Male Veteran.

Riley turned 11 years of age on March 17, 2012 and raised the bar for being *"The oldest winning Samoyed male at a National."* Just to win a National at any age is something to treasure forever!

Ryann Grady showed Riley to his Northern California Best in Show at a Specialty after Riley was groomed in the Oakland, CA airport parking lot. Jim and Riley stayed at the Holiday Inn Express in American Canyon, and a fast food restaurant served "Ono Burgers" on the menu across the street.

Friday night, Jim left the Awards Ceremony very early to read the USA Today newspaper with Riley. There was an article in the October 14th paper about Kissimmee and Orlando, Florida as travel destinations. Jim told Riley that one could spell "Ono" by taking out a few letters of "Orlando" and Jim was reminded of how Ono's name appeared just before Riley's last Best in Show. Jim remembered spending time with Ono in December 2001 at the first Eukanuba Classic in Orlando while they stayed at a time share in Kissimmee, Florida.

Before Riley and Jim left the La Quinta hotel room in Utah for the show site on Saturday, Jim showed Riley the glossy 8-by-10-inch picture of Rex of White Way in harness that Mardee Ward-Fanning had given Jim earlier that week for the Rex project. He told Riley he had a double legacy to live up to (his great sire, Ono, had won the National in 2000) and he had to go out there and beat all the rest of the 320 Samoyeds entered because he was getting too old for this show business and this was his last National. Riley looked at the picture of Rex, heard what Jim said and seemed to make a connection. He understood.

Jim used the "magic comb" four times, going over Riley on Saturday morning at the show site. That was one more combing than even Multi-BISS Ch. Seattle (Riley's best buddy and brace partner) used to get at her big shows.

Team Oakbrook had 14 dogs to handle the week of the National and Riley was the last one up. Heather decided she and Riley would either be sent out of the ring, carted off to get oxygen because of age and elevation, or walk out with a purple and gold BISS rosette.

When judge Beth Riley pointed to Riley for Best in Show, Heather picked him up (forgetting about her broken back), hugged him, and would have carried him out if there weren't so many people running up for hugs and congratulations!

Before Heather put on her armband #145 to take Riley in the ring for the first time on October 16, 2011 for Best in Show judging under Judge Beth Riley, Jim had written in ink "Mister Best in Show" on the inside of the armband, unbeknownst to Heather.

We just knew.

HEATHER KELLY SHOWED RILEY TO HIS SCA NATIONAL "BEST IN SHOW."
JIM CHESKAWICH OFTEN REFERS TO HER AS "THE SORCERESS"
AND TO HIMSELF AS "THE SORCERESS'S APPRENTICE."

Heather said during Best of Breed judging after making eye contact with her dad (Alan) outside the ring, she felt Ono's presence and looked down at Riley, the two of them became one and they were in a zone. He is the consummate show dog!

Jane Stevenson had "called" his win first, on Tuesday during Veteran's Sweeps the week of the 2011 National, when she said Riley "was pushing for breed."

Then we all believed.

Riley didn't disappoint, and gave everyone connected with his win the thrill of a lifetime!

We thank Beth Riley, Audrey Lycan, and Walt Herrmann for "finding" Riley in their ring the week of the National and putting him up. The crowd response was tremendous, and Riley thanks his "army," which started forming at Vet Sweeps on Tuesday and which seemed to be made up of a lot of his Sweepstakes Judges, Regular Judges, and the handlers and owners of his competition.

As I write this, Riley has spent an afternoon in The Presidio Chapel in San Francisco while we worked on the Rex docu-drama. He excels at therapy dog work with the Alzheimer home and Assisted Living places in Longview, Washington and is a fine breed ambassador who enjoys "Meet the Breed" events at AKC shows. He still chases that darn tennis ball like a Golden Retriever, he likes the Lone Ranger TV series (especially the horse, Silver), weighs 58 pounds, and stands just a hair or two over 23½ inches. He still does his regular "road work" up the hill to keep in shape.

He followed in Ono's footsteps, and has now left his own mark on the breed, as he made a very late (seemingly impossible at his age) but successful "Run for the Roses."

He belongs to the breed now. The ultimate show dog!

"RILEY" LIVING THE LIFE OF RILEY, AT HOME WITH JIM CHESKAWICH AND FRIENDS. PHOTOGRAPH BY JIM CHESKAWICH. COURTESY JIM CHESKAWICH.

Appendix B

"I Remember Ono"

By Jim Cheskawich

(What follows was originally written in 2001.)

Our breed suffered a tragic loss on December 13, 2001 as Ch. Oakbrook's Strike It Rich (Ono) died on his journey by plane from Orlando, Florida back to his home in California. Ono was owned by Leon and Kathy Ward and Jane and Alan Stevenson and handled by Alan. Traveling by plane is one of the hazards of being a show dog. Ono died while he was working.

Ono had just turned 4 the day before when he took an Award of Merit (AOM) and Best Bred By of Breed at the AKC-Eukanuba American Dog Classic. Ono's career was way too brief but still brilliant. He was larger than life in his accomplishments and was truly a superstar who excelled in the conformation ring as well as in breeding programs across the country.

He finished 2001 as the top male Samoyed in the United States in conformation. The grandson of a Best in Show dog and the son of a Grand Futurity Winner, he burst on the scene as the Grand Futurity Winner, Sweepstakes Winner, and Best Bred By Exhibitor at the 1998 SCA National in California. In 2000, he won Best of Breed at the SCA National in Maryland (as his son, Riley, would also replicate in 2011 in Utah); in 2001 he took Best of Opposite Sex at the SCA National in Denver in addition to Top Stud Dog honors. For a part of 2001, he was the #1 Samoyed in the country. Along the way, he picked up Specialty wins, Group wins and Group placements. He was only bred to 14 times but produced a Futurity Winner at the 2001 SCA National, the Best Puppy at the 2001 National, and multiple champions who finished or are on the way to finishing as puppies with Specialty and multiple Sweepstakes wins.

I was fortunate to have crossed paths with Ono several times over the past few years. I have read where judges can't wait to get their hands on a top breed specimen, yet I was luckier than any judge. I was able to spend time with Ono and two of his breeders, Alan and Jane Stevenson, at a time-share in Kissimmee, Florida for the last 4 days of his life. In that short time, he taught me some secrets of the universe that will stay with me forever.

I have learned from all of my Sammies, but Ono was very, very special.

He was an easy dog to get to know and love. Just a bit aloof but that only added to his mystique. He was a very handsome boy who moved effortlessly and usually answered to the name of "Onie," "Doofus," or "Mr. Doofus" although it was apparent to me that I was always in the company of royalty when I was around him.

The first night I was out with Alan walking Ono in the near dark and I momentarily forgot whom we were with. Ono's movement, grace, and presence startled me, which were pretty near perfection. I was proud to have Ono on the end of the lead in the early mornings around 6:30 a.m. as I often got up early to walk him while the Stevensons and my wife, Celinda, slept in. We would visit the flower garden and keep the feral cats a good 100 feet away as they dared not come around while HE was out for his morning constitutional. But they knew they were privileged to be in his company too and they were good sports about it.

Squirrels routinely took flight well in front of his approach. One early morning Ono jumped on a bench in Old Town Kissimmee as he had sent three squirrels up a tree for cover. I enjoyed watching him so I have to admit I let him have his fun with the squirrels as he stood on the bench with his front paws against the tree for maybe 10 seconds. When I called him off, he responded quickly without any need for my repeating the command.

Of course he had a perfect landing off the bench. I remember the sign in Old Town Kissimmee read, "No Dogs Allowed" but I somehow felt it did not apply to my friend as he was not just any dog.

Periodically we would pass palm trees on our morning walks. Being from Southern California, he knew how to greet a palm tree and what they were good for—as far as he could tell.

I enjoyed practicing with Ono in the TD Waterhouse Centre parking lot after his AOM and visit to the Meet the Samoyed Breed booth on Wednesday. I borrowed his lead and worked with him for maybe 15 minutes. He moved effortlessly and proudly. What a gorgeous head and smile. He had bone, looks, movement, and temperament! A truly stunning boy! I decided that in fairness to Ono, the Stevensons, and the Wards, that I wasn't good enough to show him in all his glory at the weekend shows in Orlando where he had already been entered.

Thus his fate was sealed to return home to the Great Spirit on Thursday.

As with other great ones, Ono died too early but his spirit lives on in his Offspring and in our memories. I got very close to Ono in my short time with him. A beautiful, proud, and graceful spirit. When he was with me alone on our walks, I felt honored to be with him and fulfilled. I didn't need anyone else. Even the early morning trips to the 7–11 Store by van to get the newspaper and coffee was time well spent.

He left his imprint on me and his spirit touched mine. I don't have an explanation for some of the things that happened to me immediately before and after his death. Alan had earlier in the week given me a picture card of Ono. After dropping off Ono and the Stevensons at the Orlando Airport, before knowing Ono's eventual fate, I was drawn to the picture more and more and sensed something horrible.

After he passed into the next life, Celinda and I scattered rose petals along his Florida morning trail route and later on our return threw flowers into the Atlantic Ocean in his memory. And the cats did return again. As Celinda and I were leaving our Kissimmee time-share on Saturday, six cats had gathered together in front of where Ono had stayed for four days. They appeared to be crying also as they too were mourning the passing of a giant of a star.

Beautiful Ono, we miss you badly and we will meet you at the Rainbow Bridge. It has been promised!

JEANNE NONHOF, JUDGE AND ALAN STEVENSON, HANDLER, WITH ONO WINNING "BEST IN SHOW" AT THE SCA 2000 NATIONAL. (JIM CHESKAWICH WAS THERE, BUT MISSED THE PHOTO OP!)

APPENDIX C

STAMP REQUEST TO CITIZEN STAMP ADVISORY COMMITTEE

 The Samoyed Club of America Education
& Research Foundation
Jim Cheskawich
Treasurer

September 22, 2003

Chairman George A. Omas
Postal Rate Commission
1333 H Street, NW, Suite 300
Washington, DC 20268-0001

Dear Chairman Omas,

This is a request to have a postage stamp issued commemorating the life and accomplishments of a former U.S. mail carrier who was the greatest working Samoyed ever, Rex of White Way!

Rex's early career began as the lead dog on Lloyd Van Sickle's U.S. mail route from Ashton, Idaho to West Yellowstone where Rex helped deliver the mail in often blizzard conditions on the 64 mile "run." This distance is roughly comparable to driving a sled team in snow from downtown Washington, DC to Fredericksburg, Virginia—without the 7,072 foot high Targhee Pass—and returning to start another run. Rex and the team were lost in a blizzard once on the mail run and it is believed that Rex used the hum and static in the U.S. Forest Service's telephone lines to bring the mail team home through the southern part of Ashton! Lloyd Van Sickle called Rex the best trail maker in snow he ever worked with and said "Rex would climb a tree if I told him to."

As background, Samoyeds are a working breed and introduced into the U.S. from Siberia through England in the early 1900s and contributed greatly in the early polar expeditions. Rex was bred and owned by Agnes Mason of Sacramento, California, trained principally by Lloyd Van Sickle and lived from 1946 to 1957 in California and Idaho. He was a purebred Samoyed who performed at the highest levels in many venues including delivering the U.S. mail, leading rescue missions, weight pulling, sled racing, parades, conformation dog shows, and expositions.

Rex was also trained to parachute from airplanes—which proved invaluable later in several very arduous rescue operations where he was used to:

1. Pull out stranded snow-bound campers,
2. Rescue 3 survivors in a downed plane,
3. Rescue passengers from a snow-bound train, "The City of San Francisco,"
4. Pull out 3 downed planes,
5. Lead teams in the Cedars rescue and Ever Valley snow removal rescue.

In 1952, in the middle of the Golden Gate dog show, Rex was urgently needed to take doctors to a snow-bound train in the Sierra Mountains and so Rex had to leave the show to be flown to Donner Pass, which resulted in another successful and very difficult rescue. Rex's value in rescue work was deemed more important than show wins and it is a fact that Rex never attained his show championship although he is behind a significant number of Samoyed breeding programs today.

In 1953, Rex appeared in "Islands in the Sky" as an actor along with John Wayne. By this point he had become an international hero, as his exploits had made him famous. Rex broke the world record in 1953 by pulling 1,870 pounds. The record was set based on his own weight and the amount actually pulled making him the strongest dog in the world on a per pound basis. This record stood for at least 30 years.

Enclosed are copies of articles from the defunct Western Kennel World journal and from Mrs. Gertrude Adams' personal collection, which capture Rex's life as a working dog more fully.

Please let me know if I can provide you with more information to help you make a favorable decision. My telephone number is (360) 225-8402. Based on a recent article that appeared in the Samoyed Club of America Bulletin (summer 2003), which I am enclosing, it would appear that the U.S. Postal Service has been very reluctant to issue stamps depicting dogs. It is believed that no stamp has been issued in the United States featuring a Samoyed, yet other countries seemingly have found it profitable to issue Samoyeds as well as other breeds on their stamps. I do hope you will make an exception in the case of Rex of White Way as he was a very extraordinary dog.

May I suggest that Rex appear along with other working, rescue, or northern breed dogs in a series of stamps, which should prove very popular with collectors and dog fanciers. Or, you may choose to issue Rex alone in memory of his contributions to the betterment and advancement of mankind. Your favorable response to this long overdue tribute to a Samoyed who, as a U.S. civil servant, delivered the mail faithfully on a regular route, among his other achievements, would be appreciated.

Sincerely,

Jim Cheskawich, Past President
Samoyed Club of America

Enclosures

183 Wieri Road, Woodland, Washington 98674
Tel: (360) 225-8402 Fax: (360) 225-3513
E-mail: samtres@earthlink.net

[AUTHOR'S NOTE: Correction for letter, previous page:
In 1953, Rex worked on the set of *Island in the Sky*.]

January 18, 2012

Citizens' Stamp Advisory Committee
U.S. Postal Service
475 L'Enfant Plaza, SW
Room 4474EB
Washington, DC 20260-2437

Re: Rex of White Way

Dear Citizens' Stamp Advisory Committee,

Several times over the past few years I have written suggesting a stamp for a Samoyed dog named Rex of White Way because of his contributions to aiding and bettering mankind. At one point, Rex worked as the lead dog on a "regular" U.S. postal run over the 7,200 feet high Targhee Pass in the late 1940's delivering mail as well as food and milk during the snow reason. Rex's trainer and musher, Lloyd van Sickle is already in the U.S. Postal Hall of Fame in Washington, DC.

I received a post card nearly 2 years ago advising me that no decision had been made on a postage stamp for Rex of White Way. In the time that has passed, we have gone into production on a docu-drama for television on Rex's exciting and eventful life from the mail run days through the downed plane and stranded train rescues, world record in weight pulling, freight and speed racing wins, pulling demonstrations at football games and fairs on the west coast for many years, and his movie and TV work with John Wayne and Richard Boone. It is estimated that Rex participated in over 30 rescues. The most famous involved delivering Dr. Nelson along with needed medical supplies by sled in nearly 20 feet of snow to the stranded streamliner, City of San Francisco, in January of 1952. The train was stuck in the Donner Pass area in the "blizzard of the century" and Rex had to be released from the Golden Gate benched dog show to lead the rescue.

While developing the Rex story line for the filming, our video graphic artist (Dawn Pasinski) developed two quick sketches for Rex that you might want to consider for his stamp. I am enclosing both copies.

Please let me know if you need more information on Rex. The 8-minute promotion feature is almost completed and I will forward along to you later.

Sincerely,

Jim Cheskawich
Past President, Samoyed Club of America

Enclosures: 3 including Rex in harness ready to move the mail.

APPENDIX D

CONGRESSIONAL RECORD LISTING

CONGRESSIONAL RECORD ... 2005

[Congressional Record Volume 151, Number 120
(Thursday, September 22, 2005)]
[Senate]
[Page S10370]
From the Congressional Record Online through the
Government Printing Office [http://www.gpo.gov/]

SAMOYEDS STRUT STUFF IN OWENSBORO

Mr. McCONNELL. Mr. President, it was President Harry Truman who
observed, half a century ago, that ``if you want a friend in Washington,
get a dog.'' That is perhaps a little harsh. Nevertheless, I note that many
of my colleagues in the Congress are dog fanciers, and the Senate is
a strikingly dog-friendly workplace. So it is fitting that we pay tribute
to a renowned people-friendly breed of dog: the Samoyed. Legendary for their beauty, friendly spirit and heroic and historic treks to the
North and South Poles, Samoyeds pulled the adventurers of yesteryear
to new frontiers.

Several hundred Samoyeds and their humans will be pulling
into Owensboro, KY, in October for the Samoyed Club of America's
``Simply Southern'' National Specialty. While I am pleased that these
noble dogs and their guardians will be visiting the Commonwealth, it is,
sadly, because of Hurricane Katrina's devastation in Biloxi, MS, where
the event was originally scheduled to be held. So the SCA Specialty
this year is a hurricane evacuee, but in addition to contributing over
$10,000 from show proceeds to animal rescue in the devastated region,

the organizers look forward to going back to a rebuilt and newly vibrant gulf coast in the future.

Samoyed dogs were named for the semi nomadic tribe which developed the breed. Living along the shores of the Arctic Ocean, north of Russia and Siberia, they were one of the earliest tribes of Central Asia. They depended upon their dogs to herd reindeer, protect against wolves, hunt bears, and even keep the children warm as they slept. Their endurance and intelligence made the Samoyed dogs prized members of early European expeditions to the Arctic and Antarctic. Borchgrevink, Amundsen, and Shackleton in the Antarctic, and Nansen and Abruzzi in the Arctic, counted on Samoyeds to explore the extreme and then uncharted ends of the Earth. The American explorers Fiala and Baldwin also used Samoyed sled teams. Most of the Samoyeds in England and the United States today are related to sled dogs from those expeditions.

Among them was Rex of White Way, who was renowned as the lead dog on the U.S. Mail sled team that used to run the 64-mile mail delivery route from Ashton, ID, to West Yellowstone, over the 7000-foot Targhee Pass. Rex was a superb canine athlete and hero. He even learned to parachute on rescue missions that retrieved survivors of airplane crashes and a snowbound train in the Sierra Nevada Mountains. Although Samoyeds are a medium-sized dog ranging in weight from 35–65 pounds, they are very strong. Rex of White Way broke the world weight-pull record in 1953 by pulling 1,870 pounds.

Samoyeds have been described as ``by nature...not a quarrelsome dog though he will stand his ground for what he feels are his rights. Each Samoyed is an individual, even from one litter. One will be very attentive and obedient while another may be more headstrong and less demanding of affection as long as he knows the house is his castle when he wants it and he owns you.''

One may detect in that description some symmetry with Senators.

The description goes on: He has a keen sense of knowing when you are happy, sad, who really loves him, just tolerates him, dislikes him and he will return his love accordingly. He is a 'talky' dog and with encouragement will voice his pleasures and his dislikes. Some enjoy jokes and ham it up when laughed at while others resent it. He will speak with his paw or nose.

Samoyeds today are still pulling sleds. They are also skijoring, pulling scooters, herding, excelling in agility and obedience trials and otherwise exemplify the ``Working'' class of dogs. As therapy dogs, they bring joy and comfort to people in nursing homes and hospitals.

Indeed, at least one Samoyed therapy dog that I know of, Gidget (Salish's Potomac Fervour), recently visited Hurricane Katrina evacuees from Gulfport, MS, who are currently residing at the Armed Forces Retirement Home here in Washington. She teams up with another Samoyed, Samantha, in regular visits with children at Inova Fairfax Hospital in northern Virginia. So these are not just beautiful dogs, they are hard-working dogs, doing great work for many people around the country.

On October 24, hundreds of Samoyeds, with their humans in tow, literally as they are prone to pull, will arrive in Owensboro. For some it will have been a harrowing journey since Hurricane Katrina roared ashore. Sheila and Walter Herrmann, co-chairs of the event and residents of Covington, LA, described their hurricane experience:

> Walter and I were hunkered down for the storm watching tree after tree fall and a tornado touch down and make a disaster of our kennels (the dogs, our own as well as the boarders were safely crated in the safest portion of our house) talking about the national is what helped us get through it.

Others involved in beating the odds and making this event happen include: Pam Barbe, Karen Brooks, Diane Dotson, Peggy Green, and Laurie Stone. I would also like to thank Jim and Celinda Cheskawich for all their good work.

Mr. President, Kentucky and I extend a warm welcome to the Samoyed Club of America's 2005 ``Simply Southern'' National Specialty.

Appendix E

Welcome to the Wonderful World of the Samoyed

Congratulations, you have just acquired a lifelong friend whose smiling face will brighten your days.

The Samoyed Club of America is here for you, and the home page may be accessed on the Internet at www.samoyedclubofamerica.org.

The SCA would like to help you to enjoy your new purebred dog to the fullest by providing you with some basic information.

History

The Samoyed is an ancient working breed, developed by the nomadic Samoyede people of Siberia. The dog's jobs included herding reindeer, hunting and hauling sledges as well as guard work. The Samoyede people depended upon their dogs for their very survival. Samoyed dogs actually slept in the chooms (tents) with their people, perhaps for additional warmth. Their exceedingly close association with humans helped to imprint a wonderful temperament on the breed with the smiling face, laughing eyes and stunning silver tipped coat.

Samoyeds know how to think for themselves and can get bored without a variety of activities and close relationships with their people. They are a dog that may chase, run and bark due to their heritage. They are not a dog to be tied out in the backyard and forgotten. Remember that a Samoyed is a working dog and is happiest when he has a job, even if it is just bringing in the daily paper.

Take Him to Obedience Class

Elementary obedience training will make your dog a good citizen and the best possible companion. Additionally, the time you spend with your dog will create a close bond between the two of you. Your Samoyed wants to please you more than anything. Look for puppy kindergarten or beginner obedience classes in your area. Kennel clubs often run such classes as a public service. The 4-H has a dog project, which is a wonderful place for youngsters to learn to work with their dog. You will meet other dog lovers and their dogs there.

Other activities to enjoy with your Samoyed are agility, herding, weight pulling, sledding, pack hiking, conformation showing and snuggling up as a couch potato. AKC Junior Showmanship competition is a good challenge for young people aged 9–18.

Health

While most Samoyeds have robust health, they do need routine vaccinations. Follow your veterinarian's advice regarding immunization and parasite control.

Feed a good complete dog food, healthy treats and do not let your dog get fat. This can happen easily to the Samoyed because his existence at a subsistence level in his native Arctic made him adapt to use every bit of food he could get.

Grooming

Your dog has that lovely white coat, sometimes with cream or biscuit trim, which is probably one of the reasons you were attracted to this breed. His coat can mat and needs to be brushed weekly and during the shedding period, daily. Puppies should be groomed regularly. Your Samoyed should never be shaved. The combings from your Samoyed can be spun and knitted or woven into extremely warm, soft garments. Toenails need to be kept short and teeth cleaned regularly.

Exercise

Your Samoyed will love to go jogging with you once he is mature. Do not force a puppy to run with you. Until he is mature, he will enjoy long walks. Leash training your puppy is highly recommended.

Identify your Samoyed with collar tags in case it is lost. AKC Companion Animal Recovery (CAR) offers a free dog tag with recovery information and a 24-hour toll-free hotline to help locate owners 7 days a week. For further protection, register your dog's permanent tattoo or microchip with AKC CAR. Call 800-252-7894 or go to www.akccar. org for more information.

Breeding

Before you consider breeding your dog, remember that no dog with genetic problems should be bred. An X-ray sent to the Orthopedic Foundation for Animals should certify breeding stock free of hip dysplasia. They should also be certified free of inherited eye diseases with an eye exam by a Veterinary Ophthalmologist and registered with the Canine Eye Registration Foundation. If your new puppy has parents that are OFA certified for their hips and CERF certified for their eyes, their OFA and CERF numbers will appear on your dog's AKC registration papers.

Old wives' tales regarding the benefits of breeding abound. They are just that—old wives' tales. You will have a healthier, happier pet if he or she is neutered or spayed.

Your dog's disposition will not change adversely with alteration. You will have a more polite pet that will not be apt to wander or leave his mark on your furniture if neutered.

Having a litter is in no way beneficial to a female; in fact, it can lead to problems, even death. It is a known fact that spayed bitches live longer and have fewer health problems than intact females.

Breeding dogs is a real responsibility. One must have knowledge of what makes top quality animals, an understanding of pedigrees and genetics, proper facilities to keep and socialize puppies,and be ready to take them back if the situation demands. All responsible breeders strive to produce dogs that con-form to the written standard for the breed. The breed standard may be found on the Samoyed Club of America's web site.

Samoyed Club of America

The SCA is comprised of 1,500 Samoyed fanciers. It is the parent club for the breed and sets the written standard, which is a word picture of the ideal Samoyed. Booklets available on the SCA web site include *Selecting & Purchasing Your Samoyed, Living with your Samoyed* and *Breeding Your Samoyed* as well as other literature.

Once a year the SCA hosts a National Specialty show, a show exclusively for Samoyeds, which is held in different areas of the country. This specialty show includes an Agility Trial, Weight Pull, Obedience Trial, educational events and the Annual SCA Meeting. There are Regional Specialties held around the country yearly as well.

Membership in the SCA includes the award winning quarterly "Bulletin," which features pictures of dogs and educational articles as well as club business.

For membership information, please contact the club Corresponding Secretary listed on the SCA web site.

SCA Education and Research Foundation

The SCA Education and Research Foundation is an IRS registered not-for-profit charity created by the Samoyed Club of America and its members.

The mission of the Foundation is to provide financial and supplementary support for scientific research and education that benefits the health and quality of life of the Samoyed breed. The Foundation funds research investigations that focus on the disorders that have historically occurred in the Samoyed Breed.

The SCA Foundation is solely supported by the generosity of the Samoyed Club of America on behalf of its members and individual Samoyed owners through tax-deductible donations.

Further information on the Samoyed Club of America Education and Research Foundation can be found at: http://www.Samoyedhealthfoundation.org/

Many SCA members also support health research for the Samoyed through the AKC Canine Health Foundation—a nonprofit charitable organization whose mission is to help dogs live longer, healthier lives. Supporting the Canine Health Foundation will help ensure a healthy future for all dogs. For more information about ongoing health research to help Samoyeds, see www.samoyedclubofamerica.org or call toll free 888-682-9696.

APPENDIX F
"REX" PEDIGREE CHART

```
Text Pedigree for Rex of White Way (USA)(W099280)
+--- Eng. Ch. Sea Foam (Eng)
+--- Am. Ch. Storm Cloud (Eng)(753910)
| +--- Eng. Ch. Vara (Eng)
+--- Peter of Kobe (Eng)(1572PP)
| | +--- Nadir (Eng)
| +--- Nadine of Kobe (Eng)
| +--- Chia of Kobe (ENG)
+--- Eng. Ch. White Fang of Kobe (Eng)(ENG.56900)
| | +--- Eng. Ch. Siberian Keeno (Eng. 1915)
| | +--- Foam of the Arctic (ENG)
| | | +--- Am. Ch. Northern Light of Farningham(649770)
| +--- Foama of the Arctic (ENG)
| | +--- Eng. Am. Ch. Tiger Boy of Norka (Eng)(702927)
| +--- Eng. Ch. Riga of the Arctic
| +--- Susie (Eng)
+--- Am. Ch. White Way of Kobe (Eng)(A299234)
| | +--- Eng. Ch. Kara Sea (Eng)(1667FF)
| | +--- Eng. Am. Ch. Tiger Boy of Norka (Eng)(702927)
| | | +--- Vandyke White Heather
| | +--- Eng. Ch. Kosca of Kobe (Eng)(1414MM)
| | | | +--- Koorali (Eng)
| | | +--- Susie (Eng)
| | | +--- Am. Ch. Zahrina of Norka (Eng) Can. CD(761530)
| +--- Kosena of Kobe (Eng)(1046RR)
| | +--- Suska
| | +--- White Chieftan
| | +--- Beauty (Eng 2)
| +--- Queen O'The Pack (Eng)
| | +--- Flitton White Knight (ENG)
| +--- Beauty (Eng 2)
| +--- Ladyship
```

Rex of White Way (USA)(W099280)
| +--- Snow Crest
| +--- Zero of the Arctic (Eng)
| | +--- Eng. Ch. Sea Mist (Eng)
| +--- Eng. Ch. Snow Chief of the Arctic (Eng)
| | +--- Mustan of Farningham (Eng)
| | +--- Eng. Am. Ch. Tchita (Eng)
| | +--- Am. Ch. Zahrina of Norka (Eng) Can. CD(761530)
| +--- Silver Spark of the Arctic(A340503)
| | | +--- Eng. Ch. Kara Sea (Eng)(1667FF)
| | | +--- Eng. Ch. Leader of the Arctic (Eng)
| | | | +--- Eng. Ch. Winter (Eng)
| | +--- Eng. Ch. Silver Glow of the Arctic (Eng)
| | | +--- Eng. Ch. Loga of the Arctic (Eng)
| | +--- Am. Ch. Ice Crystal of the Arctic (Eng)(A4727)
| | +--- Eng. Ch. Arctic Dawn (ENG)
+--- Am. Ch. Herdsman's Faith (USA)(A620363)
| +--- Jason(556197)
| +--- Am. Ch. BISS Jack Frost of Sacramento(A42650)
| | +--- Mitzi-Aura Laska(821575)
| +--- Cheka (USA)(A288567)
| | | +--- Laika's Lucky Day(664721)
| | +--- Dascha of Laika (USA)(A122763)
| | +--- Laika's Dinsche(898524)
+--- Am. Ch. Cleo (USA)(A462991)
| +--- Eng. Ch. Kara Sea (Eng)(1667FF)
| +--- Am. Ch. Siberian Nansen of Farn.of Snowland(A65303)
| | +--- Pinky of Farningham
+--- Nianya of Snowland
| +--- Am. Ch. Storm Cloud (Eng)(753910)
+--- Vida of Snowland(A72882)
+--- Morina of Taimir(958713)

COURTESY BOB HUPP, FROM ORIGINAL PEDIGREE RESEARCH WORK.
USED WITH PERMISSION.

REX AT SAN MATEO, CALIFORNIA IN 1952 AS LEADER OF A TEAM OF 25 SLED-DOGS!
TODAY, REX'S PROGENY FAR OUTNUMBER THAT...AND HIS LEGACY LIVES ON
AS A HARD-WORKING DOG AND A TREASURED COMPANION.
COURTESY JIM OSBORN.

REX SALES FORM

PRICE

All orders will include Mailing Costs, plus Tax in states where applicable. We will ship to you and/or to anyone you specify.

Hardback @ $18.95/ea.
Paperback @ $14.95/ea.

Special "Gift" Packages:
(4) books @ 15% discount
(10) books @ 25% discount

(Other discounts are available for larger book orders.)

I would like to order _____ Hardback books.

I would like to order _____ Paperback books.

☐ I would like personal autographing for _____ book(s).
(Wording to be determined by e-mail.)

NAME _____

SHIP TO _____

_____

_____

TEL. _____ **E-MAIL** _____

THANK YOU FOR YOUR ORDER!
Rex will be quickly on his way to you!

JIM CHESKAWICH
"REX THE BLIZZARD KING STORIES, LLC"
183 WIERI ROAD, WOODLAND, WA 98674
PHONE: 360-225-8402
Fax: 360-225-0422
E-Mail: samtres@earthlink.net
Website: http://dketasamoyeds.com

Thank you again!